Gideros Mobile Game Development

A practical guide to develop exciting cross-platform
mobile games with Gideros

Arturs Sosins

BIRMINGHAM - MUMBAI

Gideros Mobile Game Development

First published: November 2013

Production Reference: 1061113

Published by Packt Publishing Ltd.
Livery Place
35 Livery Street
Birmingham B3 2PB, UK.

ISBN 978-1-84969-670-8

www.packtpub.com

Cover Image by Arturs Sosins (ar2rsawseen@gmail.com)

Credits

Author
Arturs Sosins

Reviewers
John Andria

Anthony Ball

Acquisition Editors
Usha Iyer

Ashwin Nair

Commissioning Editor
Neil Alexander

Technical Editors
Tanvi Bhatt

Nikhil Potdukhe

Copy Editors
Alisha Aranha

Roshni Banerjee

Sayanee Mukherjee

Laxmi Subramanian

Project Coordinators
Aboli Ambardekar

Romal Karani

Proofreader
Lesley Harrison

Indexer
Mehreen Deshmukh

Production Coordinator
Alwin Roy

Cover Work
Alwin Roy

Foreword

Your 5-year old kid is solving puzzles and your 80-year old grandparent is playing Sudoku on a tablet. We would not have seen this 10 years ago; a lot has changed in a good way. Now we are in need of good content for our tablets and smart phones, such as games, educational applications and entertainment apps. This has also changed the life of independent developers.

The App Store, introduced by Apple, has created new opportunities for independent developers to develop their applications and sell them to users directly via the App Store. Now, Android phones and tablets are also big competition and there are many Android Markets available. Both are important targets. Many games and apps are planned to work on as many devices and operating systems as possible from the start.

We remember our excitement when we first came up with the idea: creating the best cross-platform tool to give the developer the joy of programming and giving them the way out of the native platforms. Gideros lets you function across platforms so that the development time is reduced, the overall code quality is improved, and support costs are reduced. What is more important is that Gideros reduces the entry barrier to big companies in the app market for the hobbyist.

This book is designed as a first step to help you start creating games with Gideros. Thanks to Arturs, the book takes your hand and guides you step-by-step into the art and technique of creating a beautiful game. You will find the development tips and tricks handy.

There are so many games yet to be created. I want to borrow the quote of the great Turkish poet *Nazım Hikmet*. He said, "The most beautiful days we haven't seen yet". I want to say: the best games aren't written yet. I hope many people decide to cross that bridge and start coding and creating...

Cheers!

Deniz Asli Soykurum Çetin,
CEO, Gideros Mobile

About the Author

Arturs Sosins is a developer living with his wife Anna and son Tomass. He has a Master's degree in Computer Science and even though he is working as a developer full time, he still loves coding and shares his knowledge with others in his spare time.

In his last years at the university, he started chasing the dream of creating his own mobile games for fun and personal satisfaction in his spare time. After trying out lots of different cross-platform frameworks for mobile game development, he found Gideros SDK in January 2012 and liked it so much that he decided to stick with it when developing his games.

In the summer of 2012, he founded a group of like-minded developers/designers who go under the indie label Jenots.com (`http://jenots.com/`). They released Mashballs (`http://jenots.com/mashballs`), their first game, in September 2012 and are currently working on a couple of bigger game projects.

As there was a lack of learning materials and tutorials for Gideros and writing was one of the his favorite hobbies, he started creating different tutorials on how to accomplish simple things in Gideros. This led him to create his new blog `http://appcodingeasy.com`. Due to popularity of his tutorials and the support he provided on the Gideros community forum, he became the most active community member.

In February 2013, the Gideros team offered him the position in the Gideros developers' team, where he has been working since then, while continuing to work on games in his spare time.

I would like to thank my family, my wife Anna and my son Tomass, for helping me by giving me the time to work on this book. I would also like to thank Atilim and Deniz Cetins for giving me the great opportunity to work with them and get all the inside information on Gideros and the awesomely supportive Gideros community.

About the Reviewers

John Andria is an author, designer, and entrepreneur.

He writes about lifestyle design, personal development, and career building. In his eyes app development is just one piece of a bigger picture. You can find his artworks and app development writings at `http://thewindforest.com`.

His life projects involve psychology, persuasion, and behavioral change researches. He currently helps social gaming companies to enter the Japanese market—and he understands what drives and engages the people there. His works, writings and children's books, have been translated and featured all over the world.

As a storyteller, he saw an opportunity in the mobile devices revolution and decided to experiment with this media as an indie developer first; but he is now getting even more involved as a publisher.

You can check the progress on the apps he is publishing at `http://thewindforest.com`.

> I would like to thank all the people who are changing the world one step at a time, those who build and ship, and those who share their knowledge.

Anthony Ball describes himself as a coder. He has worked in the computer industry since the 1980s. During this time he has witten games published by Capcom, Rare/Zippo Games, US Gold, Tiertex, MB Games, and Psygnosis.

He reverse engineered both the Sony PSX and the Sega Dreamcast, creating various Arcade emulators, programming systems, and development kits for them.

He created ReportComplete, the market leading end-of-term school reports system, used by around 1,400 schools and 12,000 teachers.

With the advent of Gideros, he returned to developing video games to create Bacteria™ Arcade Edition—his first game in over twenty years. It's available on iOS, Android, and Ouya.

On reading *Gideros Mobile Game Development*. Anthony said, "Nothing like this book or development kit was available when I started writing video games, I wish it had been though! It takes you from installing Gideros to coding a complete game that is actually commercially available. Recommended!"

www.PacktPub.com

Support files, eBooks, discount offers and more

You might want to visit www.packtpub.com for support files and downloads related to your book.

Did you know that Packt offers eBook versions of every book published, with PDF and ePub files available? You can upgrade to the eBook version at www.packtpub.com and as a print book customer, you are entitled to a discount on the eBook copy. Get in touch with us at service@packtpub.com for more details.

At www.packtpub.com, you can also read a collection of free technical articles, sign up for a range of free newsletters and receive exclusive discounts and offers on Packt books and eBooks.

http://PacktLib.PacktPub.com

Do you need instant solutions to your IT questions? PacktLib is Packt's online digital book library. Here, you can access, read and search across Packt's entire library of books.

Why Subscribe?
- Fully searchable across every book published by Packt
- Copy and paste, print and bookmark content
- On demand and accessible via web browser

Free Access for Packt account holders

If you have an account with Packt at www.packtpub.com, you can use this to access PacktLib today and view nine entirely free books. Simply use your login credentials for immediate access.

Table of Contents

Preface   **1**

Chapter 1: Setting Up the Environment   **5**

About Gideros   **6**

Installing Gideros   **7**

Requirements   7

Installing Gideros on Windows   8

Installing Gideros on Mac OS X   9

Installing Gideros on Linux   9

Creating your first project   **9**

Trying out Gideros Studio   10

Using the Gideros desktop player   12

Displaying graphical objects in Gideros Player   13

Displaying text   14

Displaying images   15

Drawing shapes   18

Using the Sprite class for groups and layers   19

Managing project settings   21

Automatic scaling   21

Automatic image resolution   23

Input settings   24

iOS-specific settings   25

Installing the device player   25

Installing the Android player   25

Installing the iOS player   25

Running the project on a device player   26

Exporting Gideros project   27

Summary   29

Chapter 2: Managing Scenes and Gideros OOP   31

Setting up our project   32
Handling scaled graphics with AutoScaling   33
Handling whitespaces   34
Ignoring automatic scaling for positioning   38
Creating scenes   41
Gideros OOP   42
Creating our first class   43
Gideros scene manager   47
Creating a global configuration file   49
Creating the start scene   50
Creating the about scene   55
Creating the options scene   58
Creating the settings class   60
Summary   65

Chapter 3: Implementing Game Logic   67

Implementing the main game scene   67
Using texture packs   69
Packing our textures   70
Using texture packs inside project   72
Using physics in Gideros   75
Creating physical bodies   76
Running the world   80
Setting up world boundaries   83
Interaction with physical bodies   83
Handling Box2D collisions   88
Managing packs and levels   92
Defining packs   92
Creating LevelSelectScene   92
Generating a grid of levels   95
Switching between packs   97
Creating the GameManager class   98
Implementing unlocked levels logic   101
Reading level definitions   103
Completing the level   104
Summary   106

Chapter 4: Polishing the Game   107

Adding sounds   107
Adding background music   108
Adding sound effects   111

Adding high scores **115**
　Retrieving high scores 116
　Updating high score on the screen 117
Creating animated game elements **118**
　Frame animations using MovieClip 118
　Tweening elements with GTween 121
Improving gameplay **123**
　Changing level packs by using the swipe gesture 123
　　Starting with MouseDown 123
　　Continue with MouseMove 124
　　Ending with MouseUp 124
　　Adding event listeners 126
　　Modifying code for selecting levels 126
　Implementing Mashballs magnet 127
Summary **129**
Index **131**

Preface

With the popularity of mobile app/game markets, there are also a lot of new development tools, especially cross-platform ones, that allow you to re-use the same code on multiple platforms. Gideros is a great example of such a tool.

Based on the Lua language, Gideros provides an easy way to create 2D games for both iOS and Android. With the one click on device testing and completely free of charge development, it should be one of the first choices to try out for all mobile developers.

This book provides an easy way to start developing with Gideros, explaining all its basics and how you can apply them in creating your own cross-platform game.

What this book covers

Chapter 1, *Setting Up the Environment*, provides information on how to prepare everything to start developing using Gideros.

Chapter 2, *Managing Scenes and Gideros OOP*, provides an introduction to Gideros OOP and scene management using your own classes.

Chapter 3, *Implementing Game Logic*, describes the main game implementation, from the game elements to level and progression logic.

Chapter 4, *Polishing the Game*, helps you spice up your game to make it more appealing and alive by learning different Gideros features.

What you need for this book

You will need to download and install Gideros SDK, which supports Windows, Mac OS X, and Linux (through WINE) operating systems. Installation and setup is covered in the first chapter.

Additionally, you will need some external Lua libraries for Gideros, which you will be able to obtain easily from links provided in relevant chapters.

Who this book is for

This book is for developers who are new to mobile game development or who have tried the native development of mobile games and were not satisfied with the complexity, speed, or huge fragmentation of supported platforms and devices.

Conventions

In this book, you will find a number of styles of text that distinguish between different kinds of information. Here are some examples of these styles, and an explanation of their meaning.

Code words in text are shown as follows: "So let's modify our GameManager class to also manage score for each level."

A block of code is set as follows:

```
local musicText = TextField.new(conf.fontSmall, "Music: ")
musicText:setPosition(100, 250)
musicText:setTextColor(0xffff00)
self:addChild(musicText)
```

New terms and **important words** are shown in bold. Words that you see on the screen, in menus or dialog boxes for example, appear in the text like this: "If music is on, we will set the **Turn off** text, but if music is off, we will set the **Turn on** text."

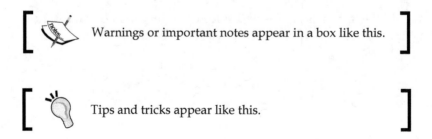

Warnings or important notes appear in a box like this.

Tips and tricks appear like this.

Reader feedback

Feedback from our readers is always welcome. Let us know what you think about this book—what you liked or may have disliked. Reader feedback is important for us to develop titles that you really get the most out of.

To send us general feedback, simply send an e-mail to feedback@packtpub.com, and mention the book title via the subject of your message.

If there is a topic that you have expertise in and you are interested in either writing or contributing to a book, see our author guide on www.packtpub.com/authors.

Customer support

Now that you are the proud owner of a Packt book, we have a number of things to help you to get the most from your purchase.

Downloading the example code

You can download the example code files for all Packt books you have purchased from your account at http://www.packtpub.com. If you purchased this book elsewhere, you can visit http://www.packtpub.com/support and register to have the files e-mailed directly to you.

Errata

Although we have taken every care to ensure the accuracy of our content, mistakes do happen. If you find a mistake in one of our books—maybe a mistake in the text or the code—we would be grateful if you would report this to us. By doing so, you can save other readers from frustration and help us improve subsequent versions of this book. If you find any errata, please report them by visiting http://www.packtpub.com/submit-errata, selecting your book, clicking on the **errata submission form** link, and entering the details of your errata. Once your errata are verified, your submission will be accepted and the errata will be uploaded on our website, or added to any list of existing errata, under the Errata section of that title. Any existing errata can be viewed by selecting your title from http://www.packtpub.com/support.

Piracy

Piracy of copyright material on the Internet is an ongoing problem across all media. At Packt, we take the protection of our copyright and licenses very seriously. If you come across any illegal copies of our works, in any form, on the Internet, please provide us with the location address or website name immediately so that we can pursue a remedy.

Please contact us at copyright@packtpub.com with a link to the suspected pirated material.

We appreciate your help in protecting our authors, and our ability to bring you valuable content.

Questions

You can contact us at questions@packtpub.com if you are having a problem with any aspect of the book, and we will do our best to address it.

Setting Up the Environment

The first thing we will do before building our application using Gideros is, setting up the environment and trying it out. We will need to download the latest version of Gideros designed specifically for your operating system, install it, create a project with some test code, and run it on both a computer and your mobile device.

As Gideros operates separately from Android or iOS SDKs and does not need them (context: Android or iOS SDKs) for testing or exporting apps, it is assumed that the user already has those SDKs installed; thus, it will not be covered in this chapter.

This chapter will guide you step by step on how to install Gideros on your operating system and prepare everything so you will be ready to develop your mobile game. This chapter will also introduce you to some of the basics of using Gideros Studio, managing your project, and running simple code.

Here is a list of links that might help you resolve any problems you might encounter with Gideros:

- Gideros Developer Guide: `http://giderosmobile.com/guide`
- Gideros API Reference: `http://docs.giderosmobile.com/reference/`
- Gideros Documentation: `http://docs.giderosmobile.com/`
- Gideros Developer Wiki: `http://www.giderosmobile.com/DevCenter/`
- Gideros Knowledgebase (FAQ): `http://members.giderosmobile.com/knowledgebase.php`
- Gideros Community Forum: `http://giderosmobile.com/forum/`

The following topics will be covered in this chapter:

- Explaining what is Gideros and why you should use it
- Installing Gideros on Windows/Mac OS X/Linux
- Installing Gideros Player for on-device testing (Android, iOS)
- Creating a new project and running it on both, the desktop and device
- Providing the basics of coding in Gideros
- Managing the project files
- Managing the project settings
- Exporting a Gideros project to Android or Xcode projects

About Gideros

Gideros is a set of software packages created and managed by a company named Gideros Mobile. It provides developers with the ability to create 2D games for multiple platforms by reusing the same code. Games created with Gideros run as native applications, thus having all the benefits of high performance and the utilization of the hardware power of a mobile device.

Gideros uses Lua as its programming language, which is a lightweight scripting language with an easy learning curve and it is quite popular in the context of game development.

A few of the greatest Gideros features are as follows:

- Its rapid prototyping and fast development time by providing a single-click on-device testing that enables you to compile and run your game from your computer to device in an instant
- A clean object-oriented approach that enables you to write clean and reusable code
- Additionally, Gideros is not limited to its provided API and can be extended to offer virtually any native platform features through its plugin system
- You can use all of these to create and even publish your game for free, if you don't mind a small Gideros splash screen being shown before your game starts

Installing Gideros

Currently, Gideros has no registration requirements for downloading its SDK, so you can easily navigate to their download page (`http://giderosmobile.com/download`) and download the version that is suitable for your operating system. As Gideros can be used on Linux only using the WINE emulator, it means that even for Linux you have to download the Windows version of Gideros.

So, to sum it up:

- Download the Windows version for Windows and Linux OS
- Download the Mac version for OS X

Gideros consists of multiple programs providing you with a basic package needed to develop your own mobile games.

This software package includes the following features:

- **Gideros Studio**: It is a lightweight IDE to manage Gideros projects
- **Gideros Player**: It is a fast and lightweight desktop; iOS and Android players can run their apps with one click when testing
- **Gideros Texture Packer**: It is used to pack multiple textures in one texture for faster texture rendering
- **Gideros Font Creator**: It is used to create Bitmap fonts from different font formats for faster font rendering
- **Gideros License Manager**: It is used to license your downloaded copy of Gideros before exporting a project (required even for free accounts)
- An offline copy of the Gideros documentation and Reference API to get you started

Requirements

The minimum system requirements to run Gideros are as follows:

- 1 GHz processor
- 1 GB RAM
- 210 MB disk space for MS Windows
- 340 MB disk space for Mac OS X
- 64-bit Snow Leopard version or later for Mac OS X

Gideros does not require the Android or iOS SDK's to develop, run, and export your app projects, thus you could build your app on Windows for both iOS and Android platforms. But you will require those SDKs after exporting, when you will want to build and submit your apps to the proper market.

Although installing and setting up those SDKs is not part of this chapter, let's examine what you need for each platform to build an exported project and submit them to the markets.

To build your app for an iOS platform you will need the following:

- iOS SDK
- Xcode
- Apple Developer License

To build your app for the Android platform you will need the following:

- Java JDK compatible with Android
- Android SDK 2.2 or higher
- Android compatible IDE (as Eclipse + ADT or Android Studio)

Installing Gideros on Windows

To install Gideros on your Windows operating system, download the Windows version of Gideros from `http://giderosmobile.com/download`. Then double-click on the downloaded `.exe` file to launch the installation wizard.

The first dialog will allow you to select the components we are going to install. You can leave all the components as selected by default and proceed by clicking on the **Next** button.

The next dialog will allow you to choose the directory where you want to install Gideros. You may provide any directory you want by clicking on the **Browse** button and navigating to your desired directory, or leave the default value and proceed by clicking on the **Install** button.

After that, the Gideros installation will start copying all the needed files and you will see the progress bar filling. When it completes, there will be a **Completed** message displayed and you may click on the **Close** button to finish the installation.

After that, you may launch Gideros Studio from your provided install location or from the Start menu, if you had chosen the default option to create shortcut there.

Installing Gideros on Mac OS X

To install Gideros on your Mac OS X, download the Mac version of Gideros from `http://giderosmobile.com/download`. Then double-click on the downloaded `.dmg` file to mount it.

After that, all you have to do is to drag-and-drop the Gideros folder into your `Applications` directory. It will create a Gideros folder inside your `Applications` folder, where you will be able to access all Gideros-related files and programs.

Installing Gideros on Linux

There is no Linux-specific version of Gideros, but it is possible to use a WINE emulator to run the Windows version of Gideros on Linux. If you don't have WINE already, you can install it using the `apt-get install wine` command or if you are using the Software Center, you can simply do the following:

- Open Software Center
- Type `wine`
- Install WINE

After that, you can download the Windows version of Gideros from `http://giderosmobile.com/download`.

Then, in the command line, navigate to the folder where you downloaded Windows installer and type `wine installer_name.exe`:

```
wine gideros_2013.06.1.exe
```

Then, to launch a specific Gideros application, for example, Gideros Studio, you need to navigate to the directory where Gideros was installed (typically, `/home/USER/.wine/drive_c/Program Files/Gideros/`) and type the following command:

```
wine GiderosStudio.exe
```

Creating your first project

After you have downloaded and installed Gideros, you can try to create your first Gideros project. Although Gideros is IDE independent, and lot of other IDE's such as **LuaGlider, ZeroBrane, IntelliJ IDEA**, and even **Sublime** can support Gideros, I would recommend that first-time users choose the provided Gideros Studio. That is what we will be using in this book.

Trying out Gideros Studio

You should note that I will be using the Windows version for screenshots and explanations, but Gideros Studio on other operating systems is quite similar, if not exactly the same. Therefore, it should not cause any confusion if you are using other versions of Gideros.

When you open Gideros Studio, you will see a lot of different sections or what we will call **panes**. The largest pane will be the **Start Page**, which will provide you with the following options:

- **Create New Project**
- Access offline the **Getting Started** guide
- Access offline the **Reference Manual**
- Browse and try out Gideros **Example Projects**

Go ahead and click on **Create New Project**, a **New Project** dialog will open.

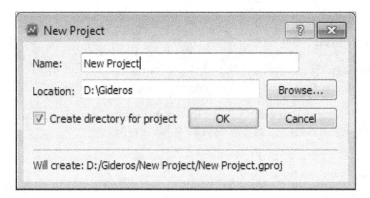

Now enter the name of your project, for example, New Project. Change the location of the project if you want to or leave it set to the default value, and click on **OK** when you are ready.

Note that the **Start Page** is automatically closed and the space occupied by the **Start Page** is now free. This will be your coding pane, where all the code will be displayed.

But first let's draw our attention to the **Project** pane, where you can see your chosen project name inside. In this pane, you will manage all the files used by your app.

One important thing to note is that file/folder structure in Gideros **Project** pane is completely independent from your filesystem. This means that you will have to add files manually to the Gideros Studio **Project** pane. They won't show up automatically when you copy them into the project folder.

And in your filesystem, files and folders may be organized completely different than those in Gideros Studio.

This feature gives you the flexibility of managing multiple projects with the same code or asset base. When you, for example, want to include specific things in the iOS version of the game, which Android won't have, you can create two different projects in the same project directory, which could reuse the same files and simultaneously have their own independent, platform-specific files.

So let's see how it actually works. Right-click on your project name inside the **Project** pane and select **Add New File...**. It will pop up the **Add New File** dialog.

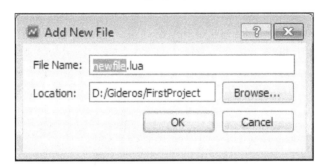

Like in many Lua development environments, an application should start with a `main.lua` file; so name your file `main.lua` and click on **OK**. You will now see that `main.lua` was added to your **Project** pane. And if you check the directory of your project in your filesystem, you will see that it also contains the `main.lua` file.

Now double-click on `main.lua` inside the **Project** pane and it will open this file inside the code pane, where you can write a code for it.

So let's try it out. Write a simple line of code:

```
print("Hello world!")
```

What this line will do is simply print out the provided string (`Hello world!`) inside the output console.

Now save the project by either using the **File** menu or a diskette icon on the toolbar and let's run this project on a local desktop player.

Using the Gideros desktop player

To run our app, we first need to launch Gideros Player by clicking on a small joystick icon on the toolbar.

This will open up the Gideros desktop player. The default screen of Gideros Player shows the current version of Gideros used and the IP address the player is bound to.

Additionally, the desktop player provides different customizations:

- You can make it appear on the top of every window by navigating to **View | Always on Top.**

- You can change the zoom by navigating to **View | Zoom**. It is helpful when running the player in high resolutions, which might not fit the screen.

- You can select the orientation (portrait or landscape) of the player by navigating to **Hardware | Orientation**, to suit the needs of your app.

- You can provide the resolution you want to test your app in by navigating to **Hardware | Resolution**. It provides the most popular resolution templates to choose from.

- You can also set the frame rate of your app by navigating to **Hardware | Frame Rate**.

 Resolution selected in Gideros Player settings corresponds to the physical device you want to test your application on.

All these options give you the flexibility to test your app across different device configurations from within one single desktop player.

Now when the player is launched, you should see that the start and stop buttons of Gideros Studio are now enabled. And to run your project, all you need to do is click on the start button.

You might need to launch Gideros Player and Gideros Studio with proper permissions and even add them to your Antivirus or Firewall's exceptions list to allow them to connect.

The IP address and Gideros version of the player should disappear and you should only see a white screen there. That is because we did not actually display any graphical object as image. But what we did was printing some information to the console. So let's check the **Output** pane in the Gideros Studio.

```
Output
main.lua is uploading.
Uploading finished.
Hello world!
```

As you see the **Output** pane, there are some information messages, like the fact that main.lua was uploaded and the uploading process to the Gideros Player was finished successfully; but it also displays any text we pass to Lua print command, as in our case it was Hello world!.

The **Output** pane is very handy for a simple debugging process by printing out the information using the print command. It also provides the error information if something is wrong with the project and it cannot be built.

Now when we know what an **Output** pane is, let's actually display something on the player's screen.

Displaying graphical objects in Gideros Player

Before we start displaying graphical objects as images on the screen, there are some things to note.

Gideros uses an hierarchical structure to hold the objects and render them on the screen with the root element called the stage.

 The variable stage is the root of the hierarchy of the objects we want to display on the screen. So anything you want to display on the screen, you need to add it to the stage variable or to any of the child elements that have been added to stage.

This hierarchy also determines the Z-ordering of the objects. For example, children always appear above their parents and, when the objects are at the same level, the later added ones appear on top.

Another thing to note is the coordinate system used by Gideros. It is the Cartesian coordinate system with (0, 0) coordinate in the top-left corner. And objects with higher y-axis value will be placed lower.

 Gideros uses the Cartesian coordinate system, where the values of the y axis increase downward, thus making (0, 0) coordinate appear in the top-left corner, and (0, 100) coordinate appears below it.

Since this chapter will include more coding examples, every time you get lost and don't know how to use any specific class (what method the class has, which parameters it takes, and what is the purpose of the class), you can get more information in the reference manual provided with the copy of Gideros. You can easily locate it under the **Help** menu by selecting **API Documentation**. It should open a webpage with the list of all Gideros classes, and also their methods, properties, and events for each class, to show you what it does and how to use it.

Displaying text

The first thing we will display is simple text. To do that, we need to create an instance of the TextField class, which would represent our text on the screen. Usually, we need to provide a font and text to the TextField class, but in this situation, we will simply provide nil instead of font. This is because we don't have any fonts yet and nil will tell Gideros that there is nothing we want to provide as font, and TextField would use the internal Gideros system font.

```
local text = TextField.new(nil, "This is a simple text")
text:setPosition(10, 20)
text:setScale(2)
stage:addChild(text)
```

After that we store the instance of TextField in the local variable named text.

We then set the position of the text we want to display. By default, the position coordinate is (0, 0), which is in the upper-left corner. But we provide a small (10, 20) coordinate offset because text is positioned by the baseline and it won't appear whole at (0, 0) coordinates, but rather be a little outside the screen.

Once the position is set, we scale the text twice as large as it is in the original, because the default font in Gideros is quite small.

In the end, we add the text to the `stage` variable, which will render this text on the screen.

Now let's try and run this modified project again by clicking on the start button inside Gideros Studio. If everything is right, you will see in the **Output** pane that `main.lua` is being uploaded again and the provided text should appear on the screen of Gideros Player.

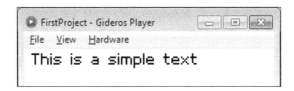

The next thing we will try to display on the screen is a simple image. For that purpose, you can use any image you have (or use the one provided in code examples); I will be using `ball.png`, which is an image of a simple football.

Displaying images

The first thing to do is to copy the image in your Gideros project folder. After you have copied the image, go back to Gideros Studio. You should see that your image did not automatically appear in the **Project** pane and you need to add it manually. So just to emphasize this difference between Gideros Project files and your filesystem, let's create a folder inside the **Project** pane, where we will store our images.

To do that, right-click the mouse button on your project name in the **Project** pane and select **New Folder**. This should create a folder in the **Project** pane file hierarchy. Now name it `images`.

After it is done, let's add our image to this folder by right-clicking on the `images` folder, selecting **Add Existing Files**, and selecting our copied image in the opened file dialog. Our image should now have been added to the **Project** pane.

You can also click on your image in the **Project** pane and see a preview of it in the **Preview** pane.

Just to sum it up and emphasize the difference between Gideros project's file management and what actually happens on your filesystem, you can see that in Gideros Studio, your image is in the `images` folder. But if you open the directory of your project in your filesystem, you will see that there is no `images` directory and your image is where you copied it to.

This is an important difference that you need to understand and take advantage of when managing multiple projects that share the same codebase and assets.

So, our image is already in the project; now let's modify our project and display this image on the Gideros Player's screen.

```
local texture = Texture.new("images/ball.png")
local image = Bitmap.new(texture)
image:setPosition(40, 40)
stage:addChild(image)
```

First, we need to create a texture representation of the image using the `Texture` class. After that, we can create the image object by providing our texture to the `Bitmap` class.

Then, we set it's position to `(40, 40)` coordinate and add it to the `stage` variable to render. If you run the project, you should see that the image is positioned at (40, 40) coordinate at its top-left corner. But Bitmap objects also have an option to position themselves using different internal points as positioning anchors, called anchor points.

For example, what if we want an image's center to be at (40, 40) coordinate. Of course we could calculate that! If we take a 80 x 80 image and want to position its center at (40,40), we need to position its left corner at (0, 0) coordinate.

But we also could simply change its anchor point to the relative center using (0.5, 0.5) as the anchor point like this: `image:setAnchorPoint(0.5, 0.5)`.

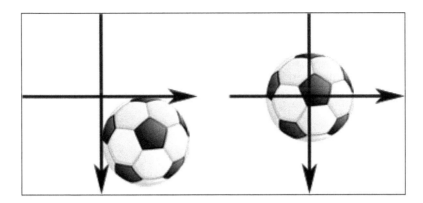

Anchor points provide an easy way to position an image relative to the provided origin point from 0 (image's top or left-side) to 1 (image's bottom or right-hand side). By default, the anchor point is (0, 0), which means that image will be positioned by its top-left corner. But when we set the anchor point to (0.5, 0.5), we say that we want to position the image by its center.

Thus in our case, the image's center will be on (40, 40) coordinate and not at the top-left corner.

And in the end, as usual, we must add the image to the `stage` variable for it to be rendered.

The separation between simple image object as the `Bitmap` class and texture representation as the `Texture` class in Gideros provides great flexibility:

- Efficiently reusing textures
- Easily changing the textures of an existing Bitmap without changing the Bitmap object itself
- Allowing us to use textures for other purposes such as, for example, filling the shapes

And again we can try and run this modified project by clicking on the start button in Gideros Studio. If everything is ok it should display the image on top of the previously added text.

I made the image to overlay the text deliberately, just to show you how Z-ordering works in Gideros. Text was added to the `stage` as a first element, and the image was added after it. Thus, if we position text and an image in the way they would overlay, the image would be on top of the text (only because it was added to the `stage` after the text).

Drawing shapes

Another thing we will try to display on the screen would be our drawn shape. For that purpose, there is a `Shape` class in Gideros, which could draw any shape from the provided coordinates that can have line style and fill style of a solid color image.

```
local shape = Shape.new()
shape:setLineStyle(5, 0xff0000, 1)
shape:setFillStyle(Shape.SOLID, 0x0000ff, 0.5)
```

First we create the `Shape` instance and store it in the `shape` variable. After that, we set the style of the lines used in the shape. In the example, by calling `shape:setLineStyle(5, 0xff0000, 1)`, we use red lines that are 5 px wide and with full opacity. An opacity or alpha channel can be provided as values between 0 (fully transparent) and 1 (not transparent).

After we set our line styles, we also provide a fill style using the `shape:setFillStyle(Shape.SOLID, 0x0000ff, 0.5)` method call. Here, `Shape.SOLID` specifies that we will be using a solid color to fill the shape (we could also use texture to fill the shape by providing `Shape.TEXTURE`). Then, similar to what we did before, we provide a fill color and an alpha value. In our case, blue and semi-transparent alpha value.

```
shape:beginPath()
shape:moveTo(0,0)
shape:lineTo(0, 100)
shape:lineTo(100, 100)
shape:lineTo(100, 0)
shape:closePath()
shape:endPath()
```

After we have set the style of our shape, we can draw something with that. To let the `shape` object know we want to start drawing, we need to call the `shape:beginPath()` method. After that, we can imagine that we have a pencil and we need to move it using `shape:moveTo` to some relative coordinate; in our case, (0, 0) coordinate. Then we can draw a line to another coordinate using the `shape:lineTo` method. In our case, we are drawing a square with 100 px wide sides.

When we've finished drawing, we can call the `shape:closePath()` method, which would automatically draw the line from a last and first point in the shape. Then, we tell the `shape` object that we've finished drawing by calling the `shape:endPath()` method.

```
shape:setPosition(40, 40)
stage:addChild(shape)
```

And the last thing we should do is to position the shape and add it to the `stage` variable, so it would be rendered.

Let's again run the project by clicking on the start button in Gideros Studio.

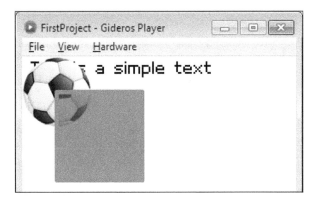

Now, on the Gideros Player screen you should see some text and an image positioned over the text, because it was added to the `stage` variable after it. And you should see a square with red line and a blue semi-transparent filling over the image (because it was added to the `stage` variable after the image). As the filling of the square is semi-transparent, you should also see the image underneath it.

There is also an alternative to `Shape`, which is called the `Mesh` class, and it allows you to draw in triangles and provide much wider functionality, such as setting separate colors for vertices and creating gradients.

Additionally, meshes are more efficient than shapes, but they are also much more complex to use (you would have to represent all shapes in triangles to use meshes) and have their own limitations, for example, mesh triangles can't be transformed (rotated, scaled) as `Shapes`.

Using the Sprite class for groups and layers

By now, we should have three objects positioned in the way they overlay each other. But what if we want to position them somewhere else on the screen while maintaining their relative positions (they would still overlay in exactly the same way)?

The first thought would be to move them separately by the same amount of coordinates. It might be ok to do so while there are three objects, but imagine if we had hundreds of objects to move; it might not be so easy or efficient to move them separately.

For that purpose we can use the `Sprite` class, which is actually just a dummy holder (without anything to render) and is meant to group other objects. So instead of adding our text, image, and shape straight to the `stage` variable, we first create a `Sprite` object to group them and store it in the variable named `group`. Then we add our objects to `group` and in the end, add this group to the `stage` variable.

```
local group = Sprite.new()
group:addChild(text)
group:addChild(image)
group:addChild(shape)
stage:addChild(group)
```

After this modification, we can move the whole group; so for example, if we call the `group:setPosition(100, 100)` method, the whole group would be moved to (100, 100) coordinates, maintaining their relative positions to each other.

This is one of the most common usages of the `Sprite` class, but there is another one, which is meant for dividing groups of objects into layers.

Now, for example, we have a need to add and remove objects in our game, but we want to add each new object underneath our current three objects, so that our `text`, `image`, and `shape` objects would always be on top overlaying any newly added object.

Of course, it may seem hard to achieve because Gideros uses a Z index based on an object's position in the rendering hierarchy, so all new elements will always be on top. But actually, it can be done very easily by using the `Sprite` object as a layer.

First, we will create a new group using the `Sprite` class and store it in the `bottomLayer` variable. Then we will add this layer below our `group` by using the `stage:addChildAt` method and providing index 1, which means first. It will add `bottomLayer` before `group`, thus making it appear overlapped.

```
local bottomLayer = Sprite.new()
stage:addChildAt(bottomLayer, 1)
```

After that, there is no need to use `stage:addChildAt` anymore, because every object you add to `bottomLayer` will automatically be underneath the `group` (because this layer by itself is underneath the `group`).

This example perfectly demonstrates how the rendering hierarchy works in Gideros, and you can experiment more with it to understand it better and use it to your advantage.

Managing project settings

Now when we have something to see in our Gideros Player, let's experiment more with a player's customizations and change its resolution to something higher, such as an iPad's resolution (768 x 1024). When you have done this, hit the start button in our Gideros Studio to refresh the project.

Previously, our group, when set to (100, 100) coordinates, was almost at the center of the app, but now it's in the top-left corner. Why is that?

Well, previously we ran our app in the default (320 x 480) resolution, but now there is a higher resolution (768 x 1024), and relatively, our positioned group is still at the (100, 100) coordinate.

But does this mean you will have to create a different app layout for each resolution? Of course not, Gideros can handle the automatic scaling for you. Let's try it out.

Automatic scaling

Right-click on your project name inside the **Project** pane in Gideros Studio and select **Properties**. The **Project Properties** dialog should pop up.

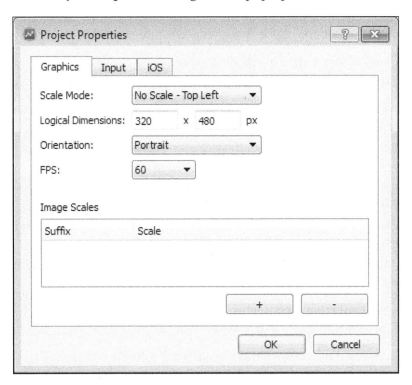

In the **Project Properties** dialog you can perform the following tasks:

- Select a scaling mode
- Provide logical dimensions in which you will develop the application
- Set application orientation
- Set project FPS

While **Orientation** and **FPS** are self-explanatory, **Logical Dimensions** and **Scale Mode** may seem confusing at first.

Let's try selecting **Letterbox** as **Scale Mode** and clicking on **OK**. Then click on the start button to reload the project in Gideros Player. If you did not have the iPad resolution selected in Gideros Player, then select it and reload the project again.

You should now see the same effect that was at the default resolution — our group is now at similar position.

So what happened? Gideros took our logical dimensions and automatically scaled it up to the iPad resolution, maximally without cropping it and maintaining the aspect ratio. That's awesome, isn't it?

I try to use the **Letterbox** scale mode in all my projects as it provides the most resistance to all resolutions, but let's see what the other options are:

- **No Scale – Top Left**: This mode does not scale the project
- **No Scale – Center**: This mode does not scale the project, but centers it
- **Pixel Perfect**: This mode centers the app and scales it with scale increments such as 1/3, 1/2, 1, 2, or 3
- **Letterbox**: This mode scales the project maximally preserving the aspect ratio and without cropping the screen
- **Crop**: This mode fills the screen completely by cropping all the content if needed and preserving the aspect ratio
- **Stretch**: This mode stretches the app on both dimensions without preserving the aspect ratio
- **Fit Width/Height**: This mode fits only one dimension preserving the aspect ratio

To learn more about scale modes, check out the Gideros documentation here: http://docs.giderosmobile.com/automatic_screen_scaling.html.

So the **Letterbox** scaling does what we need; but if you look at the image closely, you will note that it is quite pixelated and appears in poor quality.

There are two ways to handle this problem. The first one would be by applying anti-aliasing to the image. You can do that by providing the second parameter `true` when creating texture like this: `local texture = Texture.new("images/ball.png", true)`. Try it out and reload the project in the player by clicking on the start button inside Gideros Studio. You will see it looks better.

While this works great for small scaling, it is better to use larger images, for example, twice as large images for iPad retina resolution than used in iPhone. And again, Gideros comes to aid on this problem.

Automatic image resolution

Another killer feature of Gideros is the automatic image resolution selection. Basically, it allows you to provide the same image in different (higher and lower) resolutions. Gideros will automatically select the image that suits the current screen resolution best, based on your logical dimensions and the scaling mode.

To do that, you need to specify the scaling ratios you will be using in your images. This can be done by navigating to the **Project Properties** and clicking the + button in the **Graphics** tab under **Image Scales**.

You can specify any suffix you want together with the ratio, for example, let's specify three ratios such as:

- `suffix: @small, ratio: 0.5`
- `suffix: @medium, ratio: 1`
- `suffix: @big, ratio: 2`

Then create images with resolutions in these ratios and name them accordingly:

- `ball_@small.png` with 40 x 40 resolution
- `ball_@medium.png` with 80 x 80 resolution
- `ball_@big.png` with 160 x 160 resolution

If you add all those images to Gideros Studio, then while running the app in different resolutions, Gideros will automatically choose the image that suits the device best. Thus for example, in **Letterbox** scaling, the image won't be so upscaled anymore, because the larger version of it will be used automatically.

 All the example setting provided here could be interpreted as default or recommended. But you will need to experiment with your own combination of image sizes, logical dimensions, and scaling modes to achieve results most suitable for your game needs and device-resolution coverage.

Input settings

That's all about the **Graphics** tab. Now let's move on to the next one, the **Input** tab.

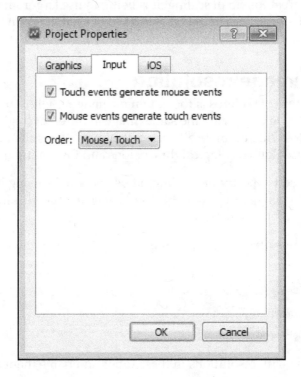

Apart from the key inputs, there are two types of input events in Gideros:

- Mouse events meant for desktops
- Touch events meant for mobile devices

The settings on the **Input** tab allow you to generate mouse events on mobile devices and touch events (with single touch) on a desktop player. So both of the events would be compatible with any platform. Also for example, you could use mouse events to handle single touches more easier and touch events for multiple touches. Thus, it is recommended to enable generation of both events.

iOS-specific settings

On the last tab, there are some iOS-specific settings allowing you to enable or disable the retina support and autorotation for a specific set of iOS devices. Due to the Apple policy, when reviewing apps, it is recommended to enable retina and autorotation either for both iPad and iPhone (if you are creating a universal project) or for the specific device you will be supporting in your app.

Installing the device player

To test your Gideros project on the device, you must first install the Gideros Player app (specific to each platform), then it will work similar to the Gideros desktop player, but without all the customization options, it will simply use your device settings.

Installing the Android player

Installing Gideros Player for Android is quite easy. There is a `GiderosAndroidPlayer.apk` file provided inside the Gideros installation folder, which can be installed like any .apk file:

- By uploading to a memory card on the phone
- By using your phone's data transfer cable
- By uploading .apk file to the server and accessing it there from the phone

Additionally, Gideros provides a way to easily install and update your Gideros Android player from this address: `http://giderosmobile.com/player/`. You can simply bookmark it on your phone and access it with every new Gideros version.

Installing the iOS player

Unfortunately, due to Apple restrictions, it is not that easy to install the Gideros iOS player to your device and it is possible only using Mac. To do that, you will have to:

- Copy `GiderosiOSPlayer.zip` from the Gideros installation folder
- Unzip and open it inside Xcode

- Connect your iOS device to your Mac (assuming you have already certified your device)
- And run the project on your device

Similar to Android, you can also get the latest Gideros iOS player project from: `http://giderosmobile.com/player/`

Running the project on a device player

Now when you have Gideros Player installed on your device, let's try to run our project on it.

To do that, first we need to launch the player on the device. Then take a note of the IP address the device player is displaying. This is the IP address we will input in Gideros Studio so it could connect to the device.

Inside Gideros Studio, you need to access the **Player** menu and select **Player Settings....**

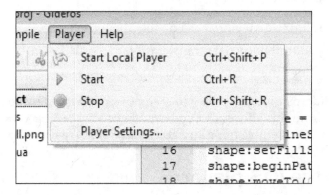

It will pop up the **Player Settings** dialog. There you need to uncheck the **Localhost** checkbox and enter the IP address displayed on the device. After that, you can click on **OK**.

The start button inside Gideros Studio should become inactive for some time and then again reactivate when Studio finally connects to the device. After that, you can simply click on the start button and the project you previously saw on the desktop player will appear on your device screen within seconds.

If the start button does not become active, ensure the following:

- Both the phone and computer are in the same LAN (connected to the same router)
- Gideros Studio is added to firewall and any antivirus exceptions you might have
- No other Gideros Studio is connected to your Gideros player (or vice versa)
- Gideros Studio uses the TCP protocol with 15000 port, make sure no other program blocks it

Exporting Gideros project

Last thing you may want to do with your project is to export it, so you could build an Android or iOS app and submit it to the market.

This can be easily done by accessing the **File** menu and selecting **Export Project**. If this is the first time you are exporting an app, you may see a message: **You do not have a license installed. Please run Gideros License Manager**.

It means you need to license your copy of Gideros (even free accounts have to license it). To do that, you must have an account with Gideros (you can register one here: http://giderosmobile.com/members/register, if you haven't done so already).

Once registered, go to your Gideros installation folder and run GiderosLicenseManager.exe.

Enter the username and the password you used when registering with the Gideros website and click on **Login**.

If everything goes well, you should see a message with your license information.

 If, for some reason, Gideros License Manager can't install a license, you can do it manually by logging into your Gideros account and accessing this page, http://giderosmobile.com/members/license, which allows you to get the license file and also provides detailed information on how to install it.

Now you can try accessing the **Export Project** option again in Gideros Studio. This time the **Export Project** dialog should pop up.

In the **Export Project** dialog, you can chose the platform to which you want to export with an option to provide some platform-specific settings. Additionally, you can select exporting a full project or checking **Export assets only**.

 A full export should be done the first time you are exporting your Gideros project. It will create a platform-specific (Android or Xcode) project with all your files inside.

After that, you may select to **Export assets only**, especially if you did some modifications to the exported Android or Xcode project (for example, installed some platform specific plugins).

When exporting assets only, Gideros will only export your files (images, code, and so on) that come from the Gideros Studio **Project** pane and will not override previously exported Xcode or Android project and its settings.

After that, you may import the exported project in the platform-specific IDE and build or run it as you would when developing the app natively for this specific platform.

Summary

We have successfully installed Gideros and tried it out. In this chapter, we created our first project and added text, images, and shapes to it. We also ran it on Gideros desktop and our installed device player. We discussed the settings provided for each app and how to use them to your advantage.

In the next chapter, we will start building our game with the basics we learned here by creating separate scenes each game should require, such as start screen and settings screens. We will achieve this by using the Gideros OOP approach and creating our own Gideros classes.

2
Managing Scenes and Gideros OOP

Now that we know all the basics, let's create our own game. We will be creating a clone of a Mashballs game, a simple 2D physics puzzler, where the main objective of the game is to drag and launch the main ball in any direction to bounce and hit all other balls on the screen. You can find more information about the game and also download it from: `http://jenots.com/mashballs`.

We will use Gideros **Object Oriented Programming** (OOP) and create our own classes, which we will be using throughout the game. As well we will learn to manage multiple scenes and switch between them, and also how to store persistent information for our app.

The following are the topics we will be covering in this chapter:

- Setting up our project
- Introduction to Gideros OOP
- Introduction to scene manager
- Creating your own scenes with Gideros OOP
- Creating a start screen for the game
- Creating an options screen for the game
- Storing persistent information

Setting up our project

Open up Gideros Studio and create a new project. Let's call it MashballsClone. While we are there, let's create the main.lua file for our initial code and also create the images folder to store our images in.

Just to make our project more maintainable, it is better to copy the files of the Gideros project in the same folders as you add them inside Gideros Studio. For example, create the images folder (and any other folder we will be creating) in your filesystem, and before you add images to Gideros project folder, copy them into the corresponding folder and only then add it in Gideros Studio. That way the structure will be the same for both Gideros project and your filesystem.

Now let's do the necessary settings. Right-click on the MashballsClone folder inside the **Project** pane and select **Properties**. Click on the **iOS** tab and select **For iPhone and iPad** as value for both **Retina Display** and **Autorotation**, which means we will support both iPads and iPhones with **Retina display** and **Autorotation**.

Now go to the **Input** tab and select to generate both touch and mouse events (if they are not yet selected) and set the order to be **Mouse, Touch**. As we will mostly require single touches, we will be using mouse events a lot, that's why it should come first. If your app won't be using multitouch at all, you can disable it here if you want. But leaving it on will do no harm.

And as the last, but also the most important point, let's set the scaling mode and logical properties; to set them let's get over to the **Graphics** tab.

Firstly, we can set the **Orientation** of the device as **Landscape Left** (as that is the original orientation of Mashballs game) and set **FPS** to **60**.

As we will be developing a game for all Android and iOS devices, we need to handle different resolutions. To accomplish that, we will be using Gideros automatic scaling and automatic image resolutions. As the base resolution we will choose an 800 x 480 display. This is also what we can set as **Logical Dimensions**.

 Please note that for logical dimensions, the first value provided must always be the width of the device and the second value should be the height of the device in portrait mode. This means the first value always needs to be smaller than the second one, no matter what orientation we want to develop our game in. Thus, fill the **Logical Dimensions** with values 480 and 800.

Next, set **Letterbox** as the **Scale Mode**, which means that Gideros will automatically upscale or downscale your screen and graphics, while retaining the aspect ratio and without cropping your screen.

Automatic scaling is a great feature for handling many different resolution types, but there are also some points that need to be taken into consideration when implementing the game. You may run into a couple of problems when using automatic scaling, and supporting as many resolutions as possible. The problems are:

- Scaled graphics
- Whitespaces
- Absolute positioning

Gideros Player's default orientation is portrait. And even if you set your project's orientation as landscape, it will still appear as portrait in Gideros Player. Think of it as a separate device. No matter what orientation you set in your project, you can always rotate your device independently. So don't forget to change the orientation also in Gideros Player (navigate to **Hardware** | **Orientation** | **Landscape Left**) when running your Gideros project.

Handling scaled graphics with AutoScaling

The first problem of course is that upscaled graphics may look pixilated. But we already know how to handle that. We will use the automatic image resolution and set up our scale **Suffix** as @2 and **Scale** ratio itself as 2.

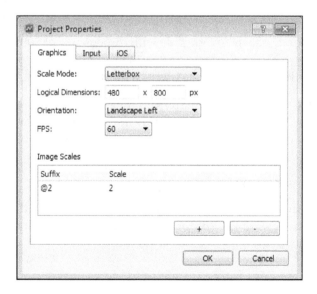

It means in addition to all the graphics we made for a resolution of 800 x 480 px, such as `ball.png`, we can also (but not mandatory) provide a two times bigger graphic (as for 1600 x 960) with `@2` suffix, such as `ball@2.png`. And in Gideros, when applying automatic scaling, it will automatically choose the closest resolution to display, so the image will be minimally upscaled/downscaled. Of course, it may seem not enough for the iPad retina resolution (2048 x 1536), but if we apply texture filtering to every graphical object we put in Gideros, it will upscale it quite normally retaining good quality.

Don't forget that in our game we will still reference everything with a resolution of 800 x 480 px, for example, object positions. That is what the logical dimensions are meant for. Both autoscaling and image resolution selection happens completely automatically.

Now that we have dealt with scalable graphics, let's move on to the next problem, whitespaces.

Handling whitespaces

As I said before, using the **Letterbox** scaling retains the aspect ratio of the screen, which is exactly what we need for this type of a game, with a specifically defined playing field. All the objects should be relatively positioned from one another, so we can complete the game using physics. If we change any position of the object, there might be a possibility that we can't complete a specific level. Thus, letterbox is the best option for this type of game. The problem is that different devices have different aspect ratios and to retain our defined aspect ratio of the game, Gideros will automatically scale our game to fill as much of the screen as possible. If it does not fill the screen completely, Gideros will center our game and leave the whitespaces.

Let's see what I mean. Create a any graphic with dimensions of 800 x 480 px, call it `testbg.png` and copy it to the Gideros folder, then add it to Gideros Studio `images` folder inside the **Project** pane. After that, let's create a new file and name it `test.lua`.

Inside `test.lua` we will create a bitmap from the texture of our image and store it in a variable `testbg`. After that we will simply add the `testbg` variable to the `stage` variable, for it to be rendered.

```
local testbg = Bitmap.new(Texture.new("images/testbg.png", true))
stage:addChild(testbg)
```

Now let's run our project on the Gideros desktop player and set the iPad retina resolution in the Player settings. You might need to set smaller zooming so you can see the entire display of the player on your monitor.

And after running it, you should see whitespaces above and below the image.

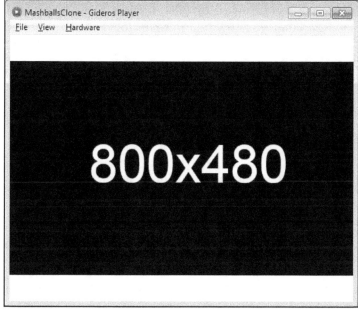

This is how the 800 x 480 graphic looks on the iPad retina resolution, with whitespaces above and below the graphic.

To deal with these whitespaces, we need to prepare a little bigger graphics, to fill in those spaces. That is why I prefer the resolution of 800 x 480 px. It is just about in the middle, between the widest and the tallest aspect ratios.

Just a little warning that we will do some math with screen resolution ratios, just to explain why we choose the background in specific dimensions. If you don't understand the calculations from the start, you can skip them and continue with the book; they will have no effect on further creation of the game.

For now, we can assume that the tallest aspect ratio will be for iPad retina (2048 x 1536), and the widest for iPhone 5 retina (1136 x 640).

So let's calculate how large a background we should make to cover the whitespaces on an iPad with a retina display.

First we calculate the iPad screen ratio as *2048/1536 = 1,33333333333*.

From our experiment we know that our game matches the width of the iPad (2048 px) but have whitespaces in the height; thus, to calculate the needed height for our background image, we divide our width (800) with the iPad's aspect ratio, which equals almost 600 px. Thus we know that to cover the iPad resolution with logical dimensions of 800 x 480 px, we need to make our backgrounds with dimensions of 800 x 600 px.

Now let's calculate the needed width for iPhone 5. Again we take the iPhone's aspect ratio: *1136/640 = 1.775*. And we know that this time Gideros will fill the height of the screen, but leave whitespaces on the left and right. Thus we take our height and, in this case, multiply it with the ratio of iPhone 5, which is *480*1.775 = 852*.

 The reason we multiplied it with the height in contrast with previously dividing it with the width is because we have used the other dimension of the ratio.

Thus, the resolution we need to make our background images for logical dimensions of 800 x 480 px to cover both iPad and iPhone 5 is 852 x 600 px.

Now let's create an image with the resolution of 852 x 600 px and replace our existing `testbg.png` with it.

We also need to position our background image to the center, so it won't get influenced by the scaling; thus, let's modify our code and set the anchor point of the image to the center. And also position the image to the center of the screen, using `application:getContentWidth()` and `application:getContentHeight()` to get the logical width and height we set in the project settings.

```
local testbg = Bitmap.new(Texture.new("images/testbg.png", true))
testbg:setAnchorPoint(0.5, 0.5)
local halfWidth = application:getContentWidth()/2
local halfHeight = application:getContentHeight()/2
testbg:setPosition(halfWidth, halfHeight)
stage:addChild(testbg)
```

Downloading the example code

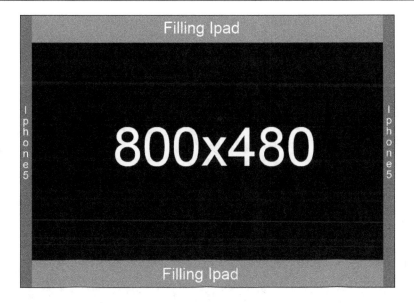

You can try running it with different player resolutions. Don't forget to re-launch the project after changing the resolution settings of the player. The following image is with the player resolution set to iPad:

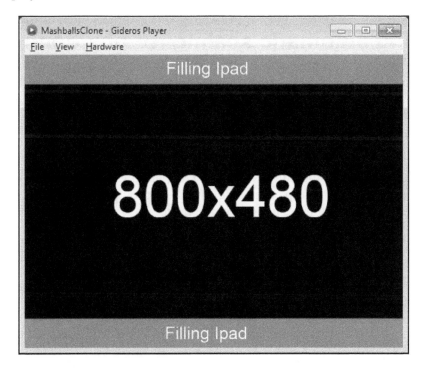

The following image is with the player resolution set to iPhone:

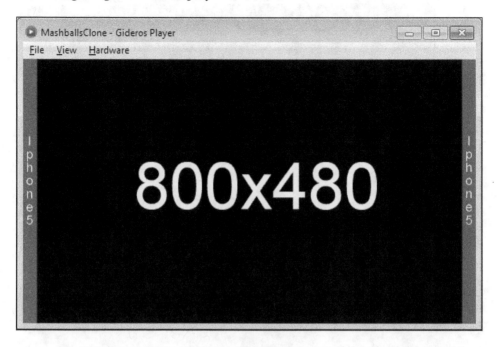

Ignoring automatic scaling for positioning

And the last problem we will need to solve is the absolute positioning of the elements. You see, while game elements which should remain relative to each other can be centered in the screen with our game, you may want to attach some other elements; for example, buttons, to the top of the screen. As, for example, no matter the resolution, some specific button should always appear in the top-left corner. Usually it is easy to do, you just set its position to (0, 0) coordinates.

But now, since we are using automatic scaling, depending on the device we may have whitespaces from the top or left side, and the button positioned at (0, 0) coordinates won't be in the top left-corner anymore.

Let's try it out. Take a simple image such as ball.png, copy it to our project folder and add it inside Gideros Studio to the images folder.

As usual we create a bitmap from this texture and add it to (0, 0) position and add it to the stage object.

```
local ball = Bitmap.new(Texture.new("images/ball.png", true))
ball:setPosition(0,0)
stage:addChild(ball)
```

The default position is already (0, 0), but I added it in the code, just to emphasize it.

Again, you can try out different resolutions and you will see that in cases where there are whitespaces, our image is not positioned at the top-left corner. Just don't forget to relaunch the project after changing the resolution.

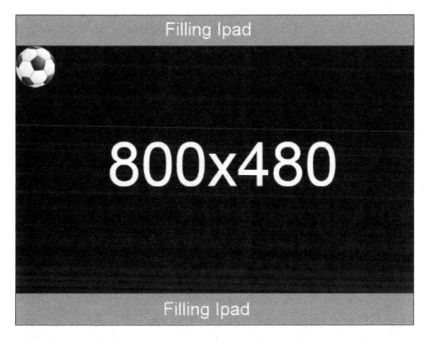

This offset which whitespaces give, is also the reason we positioned our background images to the center.

So what we need is to provide an absolute position (independent of scaling) for the image, and it is actually quite easy to do. We need to position the image with some negative offset. We can calculate these offsets on the x and y axis and apply them to our current position; thus, the ball could be placed inside the **Filling Ipad** zone.

You can get real device offset using the `application:getLogical TranslateX()` and `application :getLogicalTranslateY()` methods. But we also need to calculate this offset in logical measures, because we are handling everything in our game in logical dimensions. Thus, we need to divide this offset with the scale ratio, which we can get using the `application:getLogicalScaleX()` and `application:getLogicalScaleY()` methods.

The following is the code to calculate the offset and apply it to our image:

```
local dx = application:getLogicalTranslateX()/
application:getLogicalScaleX()
local dy = application:getLogicalTranslateY()/
application:getLogicalScaleY()
```

So let's modify our previous code to position it using negative offsets as follows:

```
local ball = Bitmap.new(Texture.new("images/ball.png", true))
ball:setPosition(-dx,-dy)
stage:addChild(ball)
```

Now you can change the resolutions in the player (just don't forget to re-launch the project each time) and see that our image will always be in the top-left corner.

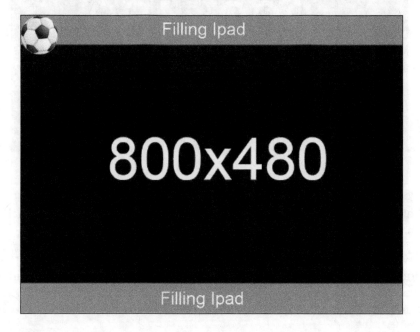

Similarly, if we want it to be positioned to the other corners we will have to calculate the other positions.

First we will need to get the screen's logical dimensions:

```
--get screen width
local width = application:getContentWidth()
local height = application:getContentHeight()
```

And then calculate each position separately:

```
--top left
ball:setPosition(-dx, -dy)

--top right
ball:setPosition(dx+width-ball:getWidth(), -dy)

--bottom left
ball:setPosition(-dx, dy + height-ball:getHeight())

--bottom right
ball:setPosition(dx+width-ball:getWidth(), dy + height-
ball:getHeight())
```

Now that all problems with automatic scaling are solved and project settings are set, let's create our first scene in the game.

Creating scenes

Now we should have the `main.lua` and `test.lua` files in our project. The first one is empty, and the second one has our experiments with project settings. But note this, if we add some code to `main.lua` too, the code from both the files (`main.lua` and `test.lua`) will be executed. That is because Gideros automatically executes all added Lua files. This might be something new even to experienced Lua developers, as you won't require every file you want to use; and it provides a much more flexible approach in handling projects. But it also has its own limitations.

For example, if all the code is executed automatically, how should we separate different scenes, we want to use in our game, in a better way? Or in what order are the files executed? What if one file depends on another one?

By default, files are executed in the order they were added, but we can assume that the execution order is random and we should not rely on it. The correct way to manage a project is to divide all your code into separate classes. This can be done by creating separate classes for every scene as well as for the objects on scenes, and storing each class in separate files. There should never be a line of code executed outside the scope of the class method (unless you know what you are doing) except in the `main.lua` file. Why `main.lua` is so special? Because it is always executed as the last file; this means all the previous files will be already loaded and there won't be any dependency problems. Thus the correct way to use global objects is to create instances and call functions inside `main.lua`. Basically, it is used to start the game-related objects and show the game's first screen.

The other special file we should note is `init.lua`; if you create this file, it will always be executed as the first file. Usually it is done to make some changes to the Gideros classes and its behavior, if needed, but we won't go that far and will use only `main.lua`.

And if `main.lua` is not enough, you can also set project dependencies, by right-clicking on the Lua files inside the **Project** pane and selecting **Code Dependencies**, you can specify which files should be loaded before loading the currently selected file. Another way to manage it is by using the default Lua style; you can exclude each file from executing by right-clicking and selecting **Exclude from Execution**. Then you will require each file explicitly when it is needed.

As we will proceed with creating our game, we won't need the `test.lua` file any more. You can either delete it from the project by right-clicking on it and selecting **Remove** or simply by excluding it from execution and leaving it in the project if you want to experiment more with it later on.

Gideros OOP

Before we blindly jump into creating new scenes to separate our game's logical screens, let's first get to know the OOP approach behind Gideros. You already saw some classes, for example, `Bitmap`, `Texture`, and `Sprite`. And you know that to create new instances you need to call the method `.new()` and pass some parameters, such as `Texture.new("image.png")`. Then these new methods return the instance of the class, where you can call the methods using `:methodName()`, for example, `sprite:setPosition(100,100)`.

It is very important to understand the difference between calling a function using a dot or using a colon. After converting it to traditional OOP paradigm, methods called through dot will be static or class methods, while methods called through colon are instance methods. It is the most common newbie mistake, so try to understand what you have in your variable when calling a method.

The internal Lua handling is actually much more interesting. The methods could be used as both an instance method and also a static method by passing the instance as the first argument.

Here we create a `sprite` instance and set its position using its instance method.

```
local sprite = Sprite.new()
sprite:setPosition(100, 100)
```

But we can also reuse the same method as a class method and pass the instance as the first argument.

```
local sprite = Sprite.new()
Sprite:setPosition(sprite, 100, 100)
```

So you see that internally using a colon means that we are passing reference to the instance as the first argument.

So now we know how to define a method and reference the instance internally, let's try creating our own class, which we will be using later on. But first let's create the classes folder inside our **Project** pane, just to separate the files. After that create a new Lua file called Button.lua inside the classes folder.

Creating our first class

To create a simple Gideros class we only need to call the Core.class() function and it returns an empty class.

Let's create our Button class and also define a constructor for it (by defining the init method), which will simply print out some text to the console.

```
Button = Core.class()

function Button:init()
  print("initializing button")
end
```

Now if we try to create an instance for our button in main.lua, it should print initializing button inside the **Output** pane, because it automatically calls the init method when you are creating a new instance.

```
local button = Button.new()
```

If it does, congratulations; you have created your first Gideros class successfully.

But since our button should be a UI element, we also need to render something on the screen. It does not have anything to render yet, but still let's try adding it to the stage using stage:addChild(button) and run the project.

O-oh, what happened? We got our first error (at least first deliberate one). In the Output pane it says:

```
main.lua:2: bad argument #1 to 'addChild' (Sprite expected, got table)
```

Why is that so?

Because not every class is meant to be added to the render hierarchy, the same as not every class can render a texture like `Bitmap` does. Those classes have something special inside them, behind the scenes what makes them what they are.

But what if we want to be able to add our class to the render hierarchy like the `Bitmap` or `Sprite` object? Then we should simply inherit our `Button` class from `Sprite`. And it can be done by specifying a so-called base class, when creating our `Button` class, like this: `Button = Core.class(Sprite)`.

Now our `Button` class will inherit all the capabilities of a `Sprite` class, which will allow its instances to be added to the render hierarchy (the stage). Additionally, they will automatically inherit all of the `Sprite` methods, such as `setPosition()` and `setAlpha()`.

Try it out and run the project now. It won't display anything, because we don't have anything to display, but it also won't output any errors.

Actually the `Sprite` class is the base class for all the objects that can be added to render hierarchy. For example, both, the `Bitmap` and `Shape` classes inherit from `Sprite` and add their own capabilities.

And that is the beauty of Gideros OOP system, extensibility of classes using inheritance.

Now let's modify our `Button` class constructor to accept any `Sprite` inherited object, as `Bitmap` or `TextField`. Then we will add this `Sprite` object to our button instance using `self:addChild`, to render it on screen. We don't need to add it to the `stage` class because we are already adding an instance of our button to the `stage` class; and as the whole hierarchy is rendered, this `sprite`, which was added to our instance using the `addChild` method, will also be rendered.

```
function Button:init(sprite)
  self:addChild(sprite)
end
```

Inside `main.lua` we will now have to create a `Bitmap` object from a texture of our file and pass it to the button or else it will output an error.

```
local bitmap = Bitmap.new(Texture.new("images/ball.png", true))
local button = Button.new(bitmap)
stage:addChild(button)
```

Now you can try and run the project, and you will see that the ball should appear on the screen. You can also try changing the position of the button, using the `button:setPosition(x,y)` method to see that our image also changes position.

Next we need to make it receive an event when we touch it. It is a button after all.

There are three kinds of events for mouse input:

- `Event.MOUSE_DOWN`
- `Event.MOUSE_MOVE`
- `Event.MOUSE_UP`

For touches event:

- `Event.TOUCHES_BEGIN`
- `Event.TOUCHES_MOVE`
- `Event.TOUCHES_END`

The mouse event in a mobile device case has nothing to do with the mouse input itself. On the mobile devices it simply represents that there can be only a single touch on the button and if there are two buttons, you can only click on one of them at a time.

It's exactly what we need and that is why we will be using mouse events. Currently, we are only interested in `MOUSE_UP` event. We could also have used the `MOUSE_DOWN` event, but due to Apple Interface Guidelines, it is better to provide the users a way to move their finger out of the button and release it without causing the click. This reduces the possibility of accidental clicks and that is why we will be using `MOUSE_UP` event. So let's define the `onMouseUp` method and print something to the **Output** pane from there.

```
function Button:onMouseUp(event)
  print("you clicked me")
end
```

No we need to bind this method to the `MOUSE_UP` event, so it will be called automatically when the user clicks on our button. To do that, inside our `init` method of the `Button` class, we will call the `addEventListener` method and pass the event name, a method that will handle the event and additional data to it.

```
self:addEventListener(Event.MOUSE_UP, self.onMouseUp, self)
```

The most confusing part here is the fact that while we have an instance method that we will be using through colon, we pass the method to addEventListener using the dot symbol. The first difference as we are not calling the onMouseUp method, but just passing it as an argument, and as you can see, there is also the third argument—self variable—which will be automatically passed to the onMouseUp method to make it behave as a normal instance method.

If you don't understand it yet, that is ok, that is the part of OOP implementation of Lua and you can use it just as a template and dive into Lua OOP specifics in context of Gideros, later.

> We could add the event listener to the Sprite inherited object because Sprite inherits from another class called EventDispatcher. And All classes that inherit from Sprite can also receive different events and have the addEventListener method.

Now if you run the project and click on the image, we will see you clicked me in the **Output** pane. But hey, what's this? Even if we click outside the image it still prints the message.

This is how Gideros mouse and touch events work. They are dispatched to all registered objects, even if you click outside them. There are reasons for that, again to create more flexible events, especially when handling multiple touches or having objects stacked one on top the other. But the fix for this is also easy. Every Sprite inherited object has the hitTestPoint method, which checks whether the coordinates currently touched belong to this Sprite object or not.

Since the event object provides x and y coordinates of the touch, we can easily implement this check.

```
function Button:onMouseUp(event)
  if self:hitTestPoint(event.x, event.y) then
    print("you clicked me")
  end
end
```

Now if we run the project again, you will see that only the clicks directly on the image provide the output and our button works as expected.

But of course, we want to specify what our button should do on the click, and we should be able to provide different actions for different instances, without hard coding the action to the class. To achieve that, we will use the same Gideros Event system we just used to receive the MOUSE_DOWN event, but in this case we will dispatch an event.

To do that, we need to create a new `Event` object with our custom name, `click`, and pass it to the `dispatchEvent` method of our `Button` class.

But before that, as we have already determined which object event was called for, we can stop it from propagating further, to save up our resources by calling `event:stopPropagation()`.

```
function Button:onMouseUp(event)
  if self:hitTestPoint(event.x, event.y) then
    event:stopPropagation()
    local clickEvent = Event.new("click")
    self:dispatchEvent(clickEvent)
  end
end
```

Now inside `main.lua` we can listen to this `click` event and provide a function that should be called when we receive it.

```
button:addEventListener("click", function()
  print("you clicked me")
end)
```

And we have a fully functional `Button` class. Let's move on creating our first scene of the game.

Gideros scene manager

Now that we know how Gideros OOP really works, let's apply it to create our first scene.

The main idea behind managing scenes is that each scene is actually a `Sprite` object (or, more accurately, an object inherited from `Sprite`), which holds all other objects to render. And there is a scene manager, which basically manages which scene to add to render the hierarchy and which to remove, when transitioning from one scene to another. That way we can control what is rendered on which scene.

Additionally, the scene manager disposes off the previous scene to free up the memory, so in most cases we don't need to think about managing memory between the scenes.

Theoretically we could create our own scene manager, but there is already one that is incredibly popular, with many effects transitions and additions, so I see no reason to waste our time and creating a scene manager from scratch.

You can download the latest version of Gideros scene manager from
`https://github.com/gideros/Scene-Manager`.

To use it, simply copy `scenemanager.lua` to your project folder and add it inside
Gideros Studio into the `classes` folder.

Now create a new folder named `scenes` inside the **Project** pane to store our scenes
there. And create new Lua file named `StartScene.lua`, which will be our first scene.

Open up `StartScene.lua` and let's create the class for our first scene with the same
name `StartScene`. Remember that it needs to inherit from `Sprite` to be added to
render hierarchy.

You can also move the button code from `main.lua` to the `StartScene init` method
and instead of adding it to the `stage`, add it to the internal scene instance using
`self:addChild(button)`. So this button will be displayed and removed together
with the scene.

```lua
StartScene = Core.class(Sprite)

function StartScene:init()
   local texture = Texture.new("images/ball.png", true)
   local bmp = Bitmap.new(texture)
   local button = Button.new(bmp)
   button:addEventListener("click", function()
      print("you clicked me")
   end)
   self:addChild(button)
end
```

Now when we moved the button code from `main.lua`, it should be empty. What we
need to do here, is to create the instance of `SceneManager`, by passing a table with
all of the scenes and keys to reference scenes and make `sceneManager` to display the
`StartScene` using the `changeScene` method.

```lua
--define scenes
sceneManager = SceneManager.new({
   --list all your scenes here
   --start scene
   ["start"] = StartScene,
})
--add manager to stage
stage:addChild(sceneManager)

--go to start scene
sceneManager:changeScene("start", 1, SceneManager.fade)
```

Note that comments in the code start with two dashes (--).

- The first argument passed to the `changeScene` method should be the key of the scene, which was used when passing a list of scenes to the `SceneManager` constructor
- The second argument is the time for transition in seconds
- And the third one is the transition type, in our case, `SceneManager.fade`

There is also an optional fourth argument, which is an easing function for transition. It requires `easing.lua`, which you can find in the same repository with `SceneManager`. All you need to do is to add it to the project, and then you can pass easing functions such as `sceneManager:changeScene("start", 1, SceneManager.fade, easing.outBack)`.

Now if we run our project, it should automatically show the start scene with our image as the button there.

Creating a global configuration file

Usually, to make your game more consistent, you will be reusing the same scene transitions, same easing functions, and simply reusing the other same values. Now we will directly provide each `changeScene` method a transition such as `SceneManager.fade`. Then what happens if we want to change the default transition type for all the provided scenes?

We have to edit all the `changeScene` calls in all the files in our project.

Thus, it is much wiser to create some global configuration file, which will hold the common values we will be reusing, so we could also change them easily.

That is why, let's create a `config.lua` file inside Gideros Studio, and store some common values there, in a simple `conf` table.

```lua
conf = {
  transition = SceneManager.fade,
  transitionTime = 1,
  easing = easing.outBack,
  width = application:getContentWidth(),
  height = application:getContentHeight(),
  dx = application:getLogicalTranslateX() /
application:getLogicalScaleX(),
```

```
    dy = application:getLogicalTranslateY() /
application:getLogicalScaleY(),
}
```

Since we did not define local before the variable name `conf`, we made it global and now it could easily access these values in other files, such as `conf.width` for getting our application width, or calling the `changeScene` method with our default values.

In the `main.lua` file, modify:

```
sceneManager:changeScene("start", 1, SceneManager.fade)
```

To:

```
sceneManager:changeScene("start", conf.transitionTime, conf.
transition, conf.easing)
```

Creating the start scene

So we already have a wrapper for the start scene. Now remove or comment out the test button code we have in it and let's add some real content. All the code we will be adding should be added to the `init` method of the scene, if not specified otherwise.

As you remember the rendering order, the things we add first will appear under the things we add later on the z axis. Thus, as a first element let's add some more background related graphics. So copy any background picture you want to use (remember we discussed to make use of a resolution of 852 x 600 px) to the Gideros project folder and add it to the `images` folder inside Gideros Studio.

Then let's create a `Bitmap` object of the texture of this image and position it in the center of the screen using anchor points and application dimensions we already defined in our `config.lua` file, and in the end add it to the scene as always.

```
local bg = Bitmap.new(Texture.new("images/bg.jpg", true))
bg:setAnchorPoint(0.5, 0.5)
bg:setPosition(conf.width/2, conf.height/2)
self:addChild(bg)
```

The next thing that will go upon the background graphic is probably a logo. Copy your `logo.png` to your Gideros project folder and add it to the images folder inside Gideros Studio.

Now following a similar process, create a `Bitmap` object from this logo and add it to the stage. You may position it however you want, but in this case I will position it slightly above the center, so we have more space for other buttons.

```
local logo = Bitmap.new(Texture.new("images/logo.png", true))
logo:setAnchorPoint(0.5, 0.5)
logo:setPosition(conf.width/2, conf.height/2 - 50)
self:addChild(logo)
```

Next we will create a `Start Game` button. We will not use an image for this kind of buttons, but rather text fields. As you remember, we created our `Button` class, so it could accept all the `Sprite` inherited objects, such as `Bitmap` and `TextField`. But this time, using `TextField`, we will use a TTF font, instead of the built-in font. And to do this you'll need to add a **TrueType Font** file to your project.

So you can create the `fonts` folder, and copy your font there. I will be using a great font by *Ray Larabie* called *Deftone Stylus*, which is free for commercial use. And you can download it from `http://www.1001fonts.com/deftone-stylus-font.html`.

Now to use the TTF fonts in Gideros, you firstly need to create a `TTFont` object and then pass it to `TextField` as the first parameter.

When creating a `TTFont` object first we will pass the path to the font and then the size we will use our font in. Next we can pass the characters we want to cache in our font for faster rendering, but that is only needed if we make a lot of changes to the text. Since this `TextField` will only hold one text without changes, we don't need to cache any characters. And, as the last thing, we can pass `true` to indicate that we want to enable filtering to this font, so it will look smooth when upscaled by autoscaling.

To make the design of our game more consistent, we will be reusing the same font in other scenes; thus, let's add the `TTFont` object that we created to our `config.lua`.

So we will add `fontLarge` to the `config.lua` file with our chosen font and 70 px as the font size.

```
conf = {
  transition = SceneManager.fade,
  transitionTime = 1,
  easing = easing.outBack,
  width = application:getContentWidth(),
  height = application:getContentHeight(),
  dx = application:getLogicalTranslateX() /
application:getLogicalScaleX(),
```

```
    dy = application:getLogicalTranslateY() /
application:getLogicalScaleY(),
    fontLarge = TTFont.new("fonts/deftone stylus.ttf", 70, true),
}
```

Now let's create a button in our `StartScene.lua` file using our previously created `Button` class with `TextField`. First we create a `TextField` object with our defined `TTFont` object. Then we set its color to yellow and create a `Button` instance with it. After that we simply position our button in the center-bottom of the screen and add it to the scene.

```
local startText = TextField.new(conf.fontLarge, "Start Game")
startText:setTextColor(0xffff00)
local startButton = Button.new(startText)
startButton:setPosition(conf.width/2, conf.height - 80)
self:addChild(startButton)
```

 Gideros uses RGB color definitions, which you need to pass in the HEX format starting from 0x000000 (black) color to 0xFFFFFF (white) color. Every two letters represent the quantity of Red, Green, or Blue channels. For example, to use the red color we use the maximum of Red channel and use nothing from the other channels (0xFF0000). And if we mix the Red and Green channels, we will get a yellow color (0xFFFF00).

And since it is a button, it should do something when clicked. Let's add an event listener to that button, so it will take us to the other scene. We have not defined that scene yet, so clicking on it will result in an error; but let's add it now so we won't forget it later.

To add an event listener, as we did earlier, we simply call the `addEventListener` method and pass the function we want to execute when the event happens — in this case change the scene to `level`.

```
startButton:addEventListener("click", function()
    sceneManager:changeScene("level", conf.transitionTime, conf.
transition, conf.easing)
end)
```

Now in a similar manner, let's add the `Options` button, which will take us to the options scene. We will add another line to our `config.lua` file now creating the new `TTFont` object with the same font, but with a smaller size, 50 px. And let's call it `fontMedium`.

```
fontMedium = TTFont.new("fonts/deftone stylus.ttf", 50, true),
```

After adding the new font with the new size, let's create the `Options` button, like we did with the `Start Game` button.

First we create a `TextField` object providing the font from `config.lua` and text. We also change its color to yellow.

Then we create a button with this `TextField` object, set its position to the left-bottom corner of the screen and add an event listener to change the scene to options.

```
local optionsText = TextField.new(conf.fontMedium, "Options")
optionsText:setTextColor(0xffff00)
local optionsButton = Button.new(optionsText)
optionsButton:setPosition(50, conf.height - 50)
self:addChild(optionsButton)
optionsButton:addEventListener("click", function()
  sceneManager:changeScene("options", conf.transitionTime, conf.
transition, conf.easing)
end)
```

And again, using completely the same procedure, let's create an `About` button near the right-bottom corner.

- Create a `TextField`
- Set its color
- Create a button from the `TextField`
- Set its position
- Add it to the scene
- Add an event listener to it to go to the proper scene

Here is the code:

```
local aboutText = TextField.new(conf.fontMedium, "About")
aboutText:setTextColor(0xffff00)
local aboutButton = Button.new(aboutText)
aboutButton:setPosition(conf.width - aboutButton:getWidth() - 50,
conf.height - 50)
self:addChild(aboutButton)
aboutButton:addEventListener("click", function()
  sceneManager:changeScene("about", conf.transitionTime, conf.
transition, conf.easing)
end)
```

The last thing to do is to cover Android-specific functionality and exit the app, when we push the Android's back button on the main screen. To do that we need to add an event listener to our scene and listen to the KEY_DOWN event, which is fired when the button is pressed.

Inside the event handler we will need to check if the button that was pressed is the back button, using the KeyCode.BACK constant. If it is, we check whether the current device is Android and then exit the application by calling application:exit().

 Note that application:exit() works only on Android and is prohibited to be used on iOS by Apple guidelines.

```
self:addEventListener(Event.KEY_DOWN, function(event)
    if event.keyCode == KeyCode.BACK then
        if application:getDeviceInfo() == "Android" then
            application:exit()
        end
    end
end)
```

And we have a basic start screen with background graphic, logo, and three buttons. Now let's add other scenes which these buttons will lead to.

 If you get an error that SceneManager is not defined in your config.lua, it means that the config.lua file is executed before the scenemanager.lua file; therefore, the program does not see it yet.

To solve this issue (and similar code dependencies), right-click on the config.lua file and select **Code Dependencies**. In the window that opens, check the scenemanager.lua and easing.lua files, which will tell Gideros Studio that those files should be loaded before config.lua.

Creating the about scene

The next scene we will create is a simple about scene, where we will simply output some information about the author or the app, or any other information you will want to output and have an option to go back to the start scene.

So the first thing to do is to create another Lua file for our scene inside the scenes folder. Let's call it AboutScene.lua.

Now let's open up AboutScene.lua and define our scene object inside it, quite similar as we did in StartScene.lua. We define the class AboutScene, which will inherit all the Sprite properties and define the init method for our AboutScene class, where, for now, we will simply print out a message:

```lua
AboutScene = Core.class(Sprite)

function AboutScene:init()
  print("inside about scene")
end
```

After that let's go to our `main.lua` and add `AboutScene` to the `sceneManager` instance.

```
--define scenes
sceneManager = SceneManager.new({
    --start scene
    ["start"] = StartScene,
    --about scene
    ["about"] = AboutScene,
})
```

Now if we launch our project in the Gideros Player and click on the **about** button, you will see our message `inside about scene` printed out in the **Output** pane. It means we have successfully transitioned to the new scene. Now let's add some content to it.

First we will add the background to the `AboutScene:init()` method as we did in `StartScene.lua`. Basically, you can copy and paste the same code by modifying the following parameters:

- Create Bitmap from image texture
- Set anchor points to 0.5
- Set the position to the center
- Add it to the scene

Here is the code:

```
local bg = Bitmap.new(Texture.new("images/bg.jpg", true))
bg:setAnchorPoint(0.5, 0.5)
bg:setPosition(conf.width/2, conf.height/2)
self:addChild(bg)
```

Similar to what we did before, now let's add the back button to the bottom-center of the screen as follows:

- Create `TextField` with medium font and text
- Set its color
- Create a button using the `TextField` object
- Set its position
- Add it to the scene

- And add the event listener to go back to the start scene

```
local backText = TextField.new(conf.fontMedium, "Back")
backText:setTextColor(0xffff00)
local backButton = Button.new(backText)
backButton:setPosition((conf.width - backButton:getWidth())/2,
conf.height - 50)
self:addChild(backButton)
backButton:addEventListener("click", function()
        sceneManager:changeScene("start", conf.transitionTime, conf.
transition, conf.easing)
end)
```

Now launch the project again; you will see that when we click on the **about** button, we go to the **about This Game** scene with the **Back** button. Clicking on the **Back** button we again can go back to start screen. So we've got it working right.

On an Android platform, there is usually a built-in back button, which we could use to go back to the previous scene, but since iOS devices do not have such buttons, we also need to put the visual button on the screen.

So since we handled the visual button on the screen, let's do the same for Android's built-in button, quite similarly to what we needed on the start screen – the only difference is that now we will change the scene instead of exiting the app.

```
self:addEventListener(Event.KEY_DOWN, function(event)
  if event.keyCode == KeyCode.BACK then
    sceneManager:changeScene("start", conf.transitionTime, conf.
transition, conf.easing)
  end
end)
```

And as the last thing, let's simply add some text to the about scene, describing our app. Firstly, let's create a small font, by defining it inside `config.lua` as we did before, now using 30 px as font size.

```
fontSmall = TTFont.new("fonts/deftone stylus.ttf", 30, true),
```

If we want to write a larger piece of text, we will have to wrap it by some width. Unfortunately, the `TextField` class does not support new lines, but there is another external class, which is built upon the `TextField` class – called `TextWrap`. You can download it from: `https://github.com/ar2rsawseen/TextWrap`

`TextWrap` supports text wrapping around the provided width and also different text alignments such as left, right, center, and justify.

To use `TextWrap`, simply copy it to the Gideros project folder and add it to the `classes` folder insider Gideros Studio. Then we create an instance of `TextWrap` by performing the following steps:

- Passing it the text as the first parameter
- Passing the width around which to wrap the text
- Passing text alignment as in this case — justify
- Passing space between lines in pixels
- Passing our new small font we defined in `config.lua`

Then we simply set its color and position and add it to the about scene.

```
local aboutText = TextWrap.new("This is a sample app, the clone of
Mashballs game, made specifically for this book and is meant for the
learning purpose", 600, "justify", 5, conf.fontSmall)
aboutText:setTextColor(0xffff00)
aboutText:setPosition(100, 200)
self:addChild(aboutText)
```

We can also add a simple heading to this scene using our medium-sized fonts. As usually we create `TextField`, set its color and position, and add it to the scene.

```
local aboutHeading = TextField.new(conf.fontMedium, "About This Game")
aboutHeading:setTextColor(0xffff00)
aboutHeading:setPosition((conf.width - aboutHeading:getWidth())/2,
100)
self:addChild(aboutHeading)
```

And we've finished our about scene. Next let's get to the options scene.

Creating the options scene

As the last scene in this chapter let's create an options scene, where we will ask our player to set the username. First let's create `OptionsScene.lua` inside the `scenes` folder and create the `OptionsScene` class inside it as we did with the two previous scenes. And let's add the background graphic, heading, and a back button (including Android back button handling) in the same way we did in the `AboutScene.lua` file.

```
OptionsScene = Core.class(Sprite)

function OptionsScene:init()
   local bg = Bitmap.new(Texture.new("images/bg.jpg", true))
```

```
    bg:setAnchorPoint(0.5, 0.5)
    bg:setPosition(conf.width/2, conf.height/2)
    self:addChild(bg)

    local optionsHeading = TextField.new(conf.fontMedium, "Options")
    optionsHeading:setPosition((conf.width -
optionsHeading:getWidth())/2, 100)
    optionsHeading:setTextColor(0xffff00)
    self:addChild(optionsHeading)

    local backText = TextField.new(conf.fontMedium, "Back")
    backText:setTextColor(0xffff00)
    local backButton = Button.new(backText)
    backButton:setPosition((conf.width - backButton:getWidth())/2, conf.
height - 50)
    self:addChild(backButton)
    backButton:addEventListener("click", function()
        sceneManager:changeScene("start", conf.transitionTime, conf.
transition, conf.easing)
    end)

    self:addEventListener(Event.KEY_DOWN, function(event)
        if event.keyCode == KeyCode.BACK then
            sceneManager:changeScene("start", conf.transitionTime, conf.
transition, conf.easing)
        end
    end)
end
```

And don't forget to add it to the `sceneManager` inside the `main.lua` file.

```
--options scene
["options"] = OptionsScene,
```

After that you can launch the project, and see that we can also go to the options scene and come back to the start scene.

Now as we want to store our player's username, we need a way to store it persistently (to keep it between application sessions), for that we will create a `Settings` class.

Creating the settings class

Before persistently saving information in Gideros, let me share a few words about the Gideros virtual filesystem. There are three different kinds of virtual filesystem directories in Gideros.

First there is a `Resource` directory, which is the same one we have been adding the images and Lua files in. It can be accessed by simply providing a path to file like we did before, for example, `Texture.new("images/myimage.png")`.

While you can add files from Gideros Studio, when the app is running, this directory will be read only. This means that you can't create any files and write anything in there from the app.

Next, the virtual directory type is the `Documents` directory, which can't be accessed from Gideros Studio, and is basically meant for usage from within the app to store all the needed persistent information. This directory can be accessed using the `|D|` prefix, so if we had an image saved in the `Documents` directory, we will have to access it, for example, `Texture.new("|D|image.png")`.

And the last directory type is the `Temp` directory for storing temporary files. You can access it using the prefix `|T|`, for example, `Texture.new("|T|image.png")`.

If you know Lua, you can easily handle file saving on your own, using standard Lua `io` and `file` objects. But in our case we will be using an abstract Lua module made for Gideros called `dataSaver`. You can download it from `https://github.com/ar2rsawseen/dataSaver` and add it to the Gideros Studio `classes` folder.

You can read more about using `dataSaver` from `http://appcodingeasy.com/Gideros-Mobile/Save-and-load-data-module-for-Gideros-Mobile`.

So now we know a little bit on how and where we could store information persistently; let's actually create the settings. First create `Settings.lua` inside the `classes` folder and open it up for editing.

Now let's create a new `Settings` class and define its `init` method. In this case we don't need the `Settings` class to inherit from anything, as we don't need to dispatch events or add it to the render hierarchy, it will only read and save values.

```
Settings = Core.class()

function Settings:init()
end
```

Inside the `init` method we will define a `settings` table with our initial values; for now we want to only define a username.

```
--our initial settings
local settings = {
  username = "Player",
}
```

After that we need a variable to mark if our settings were changed; let's call it `self.isChanged` and make an instance of the property.

```
--to check if settings have been changed
self.isChanged = false
```

Oh wow, that is new! Why did we define it as `self.isChanged` instead of simply `isChanged` as before? By defining it as `self.isChanged` we make it a property of the instance.

As you know `self` is a reference to the object this method is being called on and each instance will have a different self reference. So by adding a property to self, we make it a value, which can be accessed by the current instance.

And apart from simply defining it as local variable, which will be available only in the method it was defined, the instance property will be available in all instance methods.

Next, let's try to read if there was anything persistently saved before, by using `dataSaver` and reading our settings file inside the `Documents` directory. And then we check `self.sets`; if nothing was saved before, we set our current settings as empty table.

```
--loading saved settings
self.sets = dataSaver.load("|D|settings")

if(not self.sets) then
  self.sets = {}
end
```

The next thing we want to do is to copy our initial settings; we will do that in the `for` loop by accessing the key and value of each element in the initial settings table and checking if it already exists in our saved settings, and if not we will then copy the initial value of this key.

```
for key, val in pairs(settings) do
  if self.sets[key] == nil then
    self.sets[key] = val
```

```
            self.isChanged = true
        end
    end
```

This way we will ensure that we can add more values to the initial settings later on, and do not override the existing settings.

Now we've finished with the `init` method. Let's create a method which will persistently save our settings to the `Documents` directory.

First we check if the settings were changed by checking the `self.isChanged` property, and if yes, we reset the property to false and save our `self.sets` table to the settings file inside the `Documents` directory.

Note that although we defined `self.isChanged` inside the `init` method, we can still access it in another method, because as I've mentioned before, it is an instance property.

```
--save settings
function Settings:save()
  --check if anything was changed
  if(self.isChanged)then
    self.isChanged = false
    dataSaver.save("|D|settings", self.sets)
  end
end
```

Next, let's provide a method to get the value from settings. In that method we will simply get the key such as `username` and return the value in the `self.sets` table, which stores our current settings.

```
--get value for specific setting
function Settings:get(key)
  return self.sets[key]
end
```

And the last method will set the value of the provided key and optionally save the settings persistently. To do that, we need to get the key and value, and then we check if this value is not yet set, or if we already have the same value. If not, we set the provided value as our new value and mark the settings as changed.

Additionally, if the `autosave` value was provided, we also call the `save` method.

```
--set new value of specific setting
function Settings:set(key, value, autosave)
  if(self.sets[key] == nil or self.sets[key] ~= value) then
    self.sets[key] = value
```

```
    self.isChanged = true
  end
  if autosave then
    self:save()
  end
end
```

We should not persistently save information on every new change, because on some systems writing information to the file might be an expensive operation, which will result in the loss of performance. That is why we provided `autosave` as an option, and additionally we can call the `save` method manually when we feel we should save it.

Now our `Settings` class is done, let's create a global instance of it inside the `main.lua` file.

```
sets = Settings.new()
```

As that is done, let's get back to our options scene and add a way for the player to provide a username.

First let's display the current username. We create a `TextField` with the text `Your username is:` and retrieve whatever is stored inside our settings under the key `username` by calling `sets:get("username")`.

```
local usernameText = TextField.new(conf.fontSmall, "Your username is: "..sets:get("username"))
usernameText:setPosition(100, 200)
usernameText:setTextColor(0xffff00)
self:addChild(usernameText)
```

So now we know how to retrieve values from settings. Let's add a way to modify it. First we need to add a button named `Change it`, as we have done before.

Create a `TextField` and change its color to green, just to stand out from text. Then create a button and position it on the same line as the previous text. After that, simply add it to the scene.

```
local changeText = TextField.new(conf.fontSmall, "Change it")
changeText:setTextColor(0x00ff00)
local changeButton = Button.new(changeText)
changeButton:setPosition(conf.width - changeButton:getWidth() - 100, 200)
self:addChild(changeButton)
```

Now what we need is to prompt the player's input on the click and set it as a new username. We can do that by adding the event listener, which will create `TextInputDialog`.

When creating the `TextInputDialog` instance, we provide a dialog title as the first parameter, then we provide an explanatory message. The third parameter is the initial value in the input field, where we will use whatever is stored inside the settings. As the last two parameters, we provide names for the cancel and accept buttons.

After that we add an event listener to the `TextInputDialog` instance, where we listen to the event, which will tell us that the user has completed the input and pressed any button or dismissed the dialog.

Then we check whether `event.buttonIndex` is `nil`. If it is `nil` it means the user has either cancelled or dismissed the dialog. If it's not, it means the user has provided a value and clicked on the **Save** button.

We then take the input value from `event.text` and save it to our settings with the same username key and provide `true` as the third parameter to autosave it.

Additionally we also change the text of the previously set `usernameText` field, to display our new username upon the change, using the `setText` method of the `TextField` class.

Once the even listener is setup, the only thing left to do is show the input dialog by calling the `show` method.

```
changeButton:addEventListener("click", function()
  local textInputDialog = TextInputDialog.new("Change Your Username",
  "Enter your new username", sets:get("username"), "Cancel", "Save")

  textInputDialog:addEventListener(Event.COMPLETE, function(event)
    if event.buttonIndex ~= nil then
     sets:set("username", event.text, true)
        usernameText:setText("Your username is:
  "..sets:get("username"))
    end
  end)
  textInputDialog:show()
end)
```

That's it. You can run the project and test it yourself. You should see an input dialog pop up when you click on **Change it**. Then when you change the value and click on **Save**, it should also change it on the screen. Now even if you exit the player and start the app again, it still should have your changed value, which means it saves the data persistently.

Summary

We have successfully created the first working scenes of our game. In this chapter we learned how to create Gideros classes, by creating the `Button` and `Settings` class. Then we learned how to manage different scenes using Gideros OOP and scene manager. We also learned to use events and store information persistently.

In the next chapter we will start creating the game logic, including managing packs and level loading and unlocking, as well as adding the logic for running the game itself and creating a physics model for our objects.

3

Implementing Game Logic

We have set up our Gideros project just the way we need, using all the needed features from automatic scaling and proper logical dimensions to setting up the scene manager and creating couple of simple scenes.

Now is the time to jump into a little more complicated logic where we will manage multiple levels and packs of our game, as well as implement the game logic itself.

These are the topics we'll be covering in this chapter:

- Creating the scene for the main game logic
- Learning to use physics in Gideros
- Using Gideros OOP to manage different kinds of game objects
- Manipulating multiple levels and level definitions
- Creating scenes for choosing packs/modes and levels
- Managing game progression by unlocking new levels

Implementing the main game scene

The main game scene is where all the action will be happening. This is the place where we will have objects bouncing and hitting each other just like in the Mashballs game.

Usually, when you have an idea about the game, you don't think about the number of levels, packs, scores, and so on. You think about main gameplay and you act similarly with game development. You should jump straight to the main gameplay and create a minimum viable prototype to understand:

- Is it possible to implement it as you've imagined?
- Is the game playable at all?
- Is it attractive, fun, and something you will play yourself?

Otherwise you would have spent a huge amount of time, just to understand that the gameplay you imagined is not very usable.

That is why we will also start implementing the main game logic first.

In the start scene of the previous chapter, we created a **Start Game** button, which should lead to level scene. Let's now create this scene as we did before. First create a `LevelScene.lua` file in the `scenes` directory, then create a `LevelScene` class, which should inherit from `Sprite`. Now define its `init` method where we will add our background image, centering it on the screen with 0.5 anchor points, as usual.

```
LevelScene = Core.class(Sprite)

function LevelScene:init()
   local bg = Bitmap.new(Texture.new("images/bg.jpg", true))
   bg:setAnchorPoint(0.5, 0.5)
   bg:setPosition(conf.width/2, conf.height/2)
   self:addChild(bg)
end
```

The last thing is to add this scene to `main.lua` in our `sceneManager` instance.

```
--define scenes
sceneManager = SceneManager.new({
   --start scene
   ["start"] = StartScene,
   --about scene
   ["about"] = AboutScene,
   --options scene
   ["options"] = OptionsScene,
   --level scene
   ["level"] = LevelScene,
})
```

Similar to other scenes, we also need to handle the Android back button to go back to the previous scene. In this case, there might be more tasks we want to do before going back, such as saving the game progress, among other things. So let's make a separate `LevelScene:back()` method and bind it to the Android back button.

So, in the `LevelScene:back()` method, for now we will simply go back to the previous scene, which is `StartScene`.

```
function LevelScene:back()
   sceneManager:changeScene("start", conf.transitionTime,
      conf.transition, conf.easing)
end
```

Inside the `LevelScene:init()` method, we will listen to the `KEY_DOWN` event and check if the pressed button was the **Back** button, then we will call the `LevelScene:back()` method.

```
self:addEventListener(Event.KEY_DOWN, function(event)
  if event.keyCode == KeyCode.BACK then
    self:back()
  end
end)
```

Using texture packs

As this will be the scene where we will have many different graphics and not all of them might be used from the start, this is the best place to start talking about packing our textures.

So what is packed texture? As you have seen in previous scenes, when displaying images, we just provided a path to image to the `Texture` class and used it inside `Bitmap`, among others. While this works and can be great in some situations (especially when prototyping a game), it also has lots of downsides.

The downsides of not using texture packs are:

- Textures need to be read from a file and loaded into memory. This is an I/O operation that can be quite costly on some systems, and although Gideros caches textures and does not need to read and load it again for some time, it is still not an efficient solution to load each file separately.

- Also, this operation is not asynchronous, which means if you try to load a large graphic, it will pause your game for a while, but even if it is a half second time, it would still be noticeable and will feel like lag to players.

- There is also a difference in how these textures are processed when displayed. It is much easier for the graphics processor to handle single bigger texture rather than switching between multiple small textures, thus it performs more efficiently when we use smaller number of files.

So for all these three points, there is one solution—to pack all your graphics into a single file, which would contain all the needed graphics. After this pack is loaded, display only specific regions of the whole pack as a texture provided to the `Bitmap` class.

Of course, as usual, this approach has its own downsides. Loading one bigger file at the start will cause a longer initial load time, but it is still better than small lags throughout the game when loading each file individually.

Also, you might be tempted to pack all textures of the whole game in one pack, which is really a bad idea. It might seem more efficient to do that, but in the end you need memory to store it all and remember we are creating a mobile game, and usually mobile devices have limitations on this memory, so your game will crash on all the devices that don't have enough memory.

That is why the best way is to take the middle ground. I usually try to separate the texture packs between scenes, creating a new texture pack for each scene. If there are graphics that repeat frequently between scenes, I usually create one global pack to be used in the entire game. I find to be the best approach to managing graphical assets in Gideros.

Packing our textures

So how do you actually pack the textures into a single one? And then again use only a portion of the texture? Sounds like a really complicated job. Fortunately in Gideros, it is made easy, firstly by using Gideros Texture Packer to combine all the graphics in one and after that using the `TexturePack` class to use them all separately in your scene.

So let's try it out. First go to your project directory (not from Gideros Studio, but rather explicitly to the project folder on your computer) and create a folder named `texturepacks`. This is where we will be storing our packed textures and their projects. In the `texturepacks` directory, create another directory named `sources`. We will be storing the source files we packed there. We won't be using these sources in the Gideros project itself, but we may need them if we want to update the packed texture, by adding, for example, new graphics files, or replacing existing ones.

Once that is done, copy the images you want to combine in to the `sources` folder inside the `texturepack` directory. In our case, these will be the images of game elements and buttons used on game level scene.

Then go to Gideros installation directory and open `GiderosTexturePacker`.

In the **Texture Packer** window, click on **File** in the upper-left menu and select **New Project**; a **New Project** dialog should pop up. Let's name the project `LevelScene` and save it in the `texturepacks` directory in our Gideros project folder. You can uncheck the **Create directory for project** option as we can keep all the texture packs in the same folder.

When that is set, click on **OK**.

Now, quite similar to Gideros Studio, right-click on **LevelScene** in the **Project** pane and select **Add Existing Files...**. Then navigate to your Gideros project in `texturepacks | sources` directory where you have copied all images, and select them all, and click on **Open**.

Texture Packer will automatically combine your images into the smallest and the closest possible dimension of 2^n size (just another trick to make processing of textures more efficient). An example of a packed texture is shown in the following screenshot:

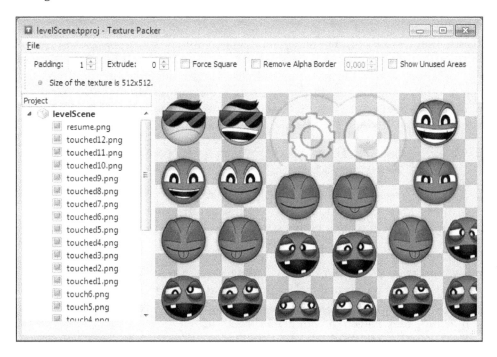

Now save the project by clicking on **File** and selecting **Save Project**. Then we need to export the combined texture by clicking on **File** and selecting **Export Texture...**, it should offer the same directory we decided to save our project in – the `texturepacks` directory. If it's not, you should change it to your Gideros project's `texturepacks` directory and click on **Save** to export the texture.

You should now have three files inside the `texturepacks` directory called `LevelScene.png`, `LevelScene.txt`, and `LevelScene.tpproj`. The file `LevelScene.tpproj` contains the texture packer project and if you want to edit the packed texture, you should open **Texture Packer** and open this project file in it.

The other two files (LevelScene.png and LevelScene.txt) are the ones we will have to include in our Gideros project. The file LevelScene.png contains the combined textures themselves and LevelScene.txt contains the information on how to separate those packed textures.

Using texture packs inside project

So now when we have our textures packed, how do we use them in our Gideros project? First we need to create the texturepacks directory in Gideros Studio and add both the files (LevelScene.png and LevelScene.txt) to this folder.

Then let's load them using the TexturePack class and save it as self.g, an instance property of our scene instance. We can do that by creating an instance of the TexturePack class and providing path to file with information about texture and path to file, which is a texture pack itself. We also provide the third parameter as true, to indicate that we want to smooth our textures when scaling. Add the following code line to the LevelScene:init() method:

```
self.g = TexturePack.new("texturepacks/LevelScene.txt",
    "texturepacks/LevelScene.png", true)
```

Now the whole texture pack is stored inside the self.g variable and we can use these textures, pretty similar to how we used separate graphic files. Let's create a restart button that will simply go back to this same level scene and thus restart our game.

So at first we create a Bitmap object by calling self.g:getTextureRegion and passing the name of the source file. This will create the Bitmap object with the source file texture. It is really that easy, we reference textures packed in single pack by the same file name they had in the sources directory.

Then we create a Button instance and provide Bitmap to it. We then position this button to the bottom-left side of the screen, as we learned before, by using absolute position offsets stored in the config.dx and config.dy variables and add this button to our scene.

The last thing we need to do is to add event listener that will go to the same level scene on button click.

```
local restart = Bitmap.new(self.g:getTextureRegion("restart.png"))
local restartButton = Button.new(restart)
restartButton:setPosition(-conf.dx, conf.dy + conf.height -
    restartButton:getHeight())
self:addChild(restartButton)
restartButton:addEventListener("click", function()
```

```
sceneManager:changeScene("level", conf.transitionTime,
    conf.transition, conf.easing)
end)
```

And we have our restart button. Let's also implement the menu button that will pause the game and open up a menu for us to do something.

First let's implement the `LevelScene:createMenu()` method, which will create our menu object and return it.

```
function LevelScene:createMenu()
end
```

So, in this method we will first dim the screen by using a semi-transparent black-filled `Shape` object. Quite similar to what we did in the first chapter, we simply create a `Shape` instance, define its fill as black semi-transparent color and indicate we want to draw by calling the `beginPath()` method. Then we simply draw by considering absolute offset too, so we dim the whole screen. After we finish drawing, we close the drawn path and call the `endPath()` method.

```
local menu = Shape.new()
menu:setFillStyle(Shape.SOLID, 0x000000, 0.5)
menu:beginPath()
menu:moveTo(-conf.dx,-conf.dy)
menu:lineTo(-conf.dx, conf.height + conf.dy)
menu:lineTo(conf.width + conf.dy, conf.height + conf.dy)
menu:lineTo(conf.width + conf.dy, -conf.dy)
menu:closePath()
menu:endPath()
```

Next, since we want to create a completely separate layer, we want to disable all the possible mouse and touch inputs below the dimmed layer, so they won't affect the game. Thus we need to add event callbacks for all possible events and call the `e:stopPropagation()` method to stop events from propagating further.

```
--disable input events
menu:addEventListener(Event.MOUSE_DOWN, function(e)
    e:stopPropagation() end)
menu:addEventListener(Event.MOUSE_MOVE, function(e)
    e:stopPropagation() end)
menu:addEventListener(Event.MOUSE_UP, function(e)
    e:stopPropagation() end)
menu:addEventListener(Event.TOUCHES_BEGIN, function(e)
    e:stopPropagation() end)
```

```
menu:addEventListener(Event.TOUCHES_MOVE, function(e)
  e:stopPropagation() end)
menu:addEventListener(Event.TOUCHES_END, function(e)
  e:stopPropagation() end)
```

In the end we simply need to return the created menu overlay.

```
return menu
```

Now, when we create the menu layer, let's define the method that will open it up.

In this method, we will set the flag `self.paused` to `true`, to indicate that the game is paused. Then we will check if the `self.menu` property is not yet defined and if it's not, then we will create a new menu layer and store it in property. Then we will simply add it to the scene.

In this case we only have to create the menu layer once and re-use the same menu layer we have stored in the `self.menu` property.

```
function LevelScene:openMenu()
  self.paused = true
  if not self.menu then
    self.menu = self:createMenu()
  end
  self:addChild(self.menu)
end
```

Now inside the `LevelScene:init()` method, let's add a button to open the menu. We get a menu graphic from our packed texture and create a `Button` class instance from it. Then we position it in the bottom-right corner, considering the `conf.dx` and `conf.dy` offsets, and add an event listener to it to open up the menu on click.

```
local menu = Bitmap.new(self.g:getTextureRegion("menu.png"))
local menuButton = Button.new(menu)
menuButton:setPosition(conf.dx + conf.width -
  menuButton:getWidth(), conf.dy + conf.height -
  menuButton:getHeight())
self:addChild(menuButton)
menuButton:addEventListener("click", function(self)
  self:openMenu()
end, self)
```

You can try and launch the project and it should open up the semi-transparent black overlay over the whole screen.

Now we can add buttons to this menu layer. Let's simply create a resume button, but you could also add a restart button, and go back to the main `StartScene`, and so on.

Inside on the resume button click event, we would need to unpause the game and hide the menu overlay. So let's define the `LevelScene:closeMenu()` method first, where we simply remove the `self.menu` overlay from scene and change our `self.paused` flag to `false`.

```
function LevelScene:closeMenu()
  self:removeChild(self.menu)
  self.paused = false
end
```

Now we can add a **Resume** button in the `LevelScene:createMenu()` method, just before returning the menu object. We create an image from packed texture and give it to our `Button` class instance, then we position this button and add an event listener to call the `closeMenu()` method. We add this button to our menu layer.

```
--add buttons
local resume = Bitmap.new(self.g:getTextureRegion("resume.png"))
resume:setAnchorPoint(0.5, 0.5)
local resumeButton = Button.new(resume)
resumeButton:setPosition(conf.width/2, 100)
resumeButton:addEventListener("click", self.closeMenu, self)
menu:addChild(resumeButton)
```

Now you can run the project again and try opening and closing the menu overlay using menu and resume buttons.

Using physics in Gideros

We have our textures packed and we know how to use them. Now comes the most fun part. Let's set up everything we need to use physics engine, which will emulate gravity and collisions for us. The physics engine Gideros uses is called Box2D.

 Box2D is a 2-dimensional physics engine created by Erin Catto and is released under zlib license, which means it can be used free of charge for any purpose, including commercial applications. Besides, being straightforward and easy to understand, ability to use it for commercial projects might be one of the main reasons why it became so popular.

First, to tell Gideros that we want to use physics engine, we need to require it. So let's put `require "box2d"` in the beginning of the `main.lua` file.

Then we need to modify the `LevelScene.lua` file. First, inside the `LevelScene:init` method, we should create our new physics world by providing what type of gravity we want to use in it.

Gravity is defined as vector which represents direction of acceleration. This vector is defined by two values: x and y. The variable x represents gravity on the x axis; if value is positive, objects would fall to the right side and if value is negative, objects would fall to the left side. The same rule applies to the y variable on the y axis. If you'd provide equal values to x and y, for example, 10, then objects would fall in the right-bottom corner. The higher the value, greater is the acceleration. Zero values would define no gravity, which would fit for games such as Billiards. We will be using real-world gravity or standard acceleration due to free fall, which is 9.8 m/s^2.

We will provide a third parameter as `true`, which indicates that we want to allow physical bodies to sleep and it is a more efficient way to use the physics engine. Basically, in most cases you would want to allow physical bodies to sleep.

After creating the world, we will save it as the instance property, so we can access it through any method.

```
--create world instance
self.world = b2.World.new(0, 9.8, true)
```

Next we will set up the debug drawing of physics objects, so we could see how physical objects actually move, and thus debug if that is something different to what we want.

For that, inside the same `init` method, we will create a `DebugDraw` layer and add it to our scene.

```
--set up debug drawing
local debugDraw = b2.DebugDraw.new()
self.world:setDebugDraw(debugDraw)
self:addChild(debugDraw)
```

Creating physical bodies

Now when that is set up, let's create our first physical object and try to see how it moves.

Let's create new folder objects inside our project in Gideros Studio, where we will put all files related to our game objects.

Then create the `MainBall.lua` file inside that directory and create a `MainBall` class in it, which inherits from `Sprite`.

```
MainBall = Core.class(Sprite)
```

Then let's define the `init` method of our `MainBall` class. It should accept three arguments, `level`, the reference to scene instance, and x and y, the position where it should be placed on the scene. We will save the reference to the scene as a `self.level` instance property.

```
function MainBall:init(level, x, y)
  self.level = level
  self:setPosition(x,y)
end
```

Now inside `MainBall:init`, let's add the image to represent our main ball. We will create the `Bitmap` object from our packed texture and set its anchor point to a value of 0.5. Setting 0.5 as anchor point value is mandatory because physical bodies will also reference to the center of the ball and we need both the coordinates (physical body and our `MainBall` object) to match.

After that we simply add this `bitmap` to our `MainBall` object.

```
--create bitmap object from ball graphic
self.bitmap =
  Bitmap.new(self.level.g:getTextureRegion("main1.png"))
--reference center of the ball for positioning
self.bitmap:setAnchorPoint(0.5,0.5)
self:addChild(self.bitmap)
```

Now we need to create a physical body of same size and shape. First let's calculate the radius of the ball by taking the image's width and divide it by 2.

```
--get radius
local radius = self.bitmap:getWidth()/2
```

Then we can create a body object by calling the `world:createBody` method and passing body type. There are three possible body types: static, kinematic, and dynamic.

A static body does not move by physics rules defined in your world, it acts as if it has infinite mass (it can't be moved by other objects colliding with it), it can only be moved by directly setting its position in code.

Kinematic body is similar to static body, it also has infinite mass and does not abide by physics rules, but in contrast to static body, it has velocity. You can define the speed with which it will move, and its trajectory won't be changed because of other colliding bodies.

A dynamic body completely abides by all laws of physics, changes trajectory on collisions, and so on. You can also apply different forces to dynamic objects. It is exactly what we want from this object, that's why we will provide the b2.DYNAMIC_ BODY value which indicates that we want a dynamic body.

```
--create box2d physical object
local body = self.level.world:createBody{type = b2.DYNAMIC_BODY}
```

Physical bodies do not relate to render hierarchy or relative positions. They have their own world in which they operate, that is why the first thing to do is to copy the current MainBall object's status to the physical body. We copy the position and angle it is currently in. Note that Gideros uses angles in degrees, but box2D uses radians; thus we need to convert our angles from degrees to radians.

```
body:setPosition(self:getPosition())
body:setAngle(math.rad(self:getRotation()))
```

After that, we need to create the shape of the body. There are different variations of it, such as PolygonShape for defining polygons or ChainShape for defining terrains, and so on. But in this situation we are creating a ball, thus we need CircleShape. We create it by providing it's center coordinates, which will be (0,0) for the shape's center and radius of the circle.

```
local circle = b2.CircleShape.new(0, 0, radius)
```

When we have defined a shape, we will create a fixture with the specified shape and other physical properties such as:

- Density: It defines mass of the object calculated based on dimensions and density
- Friction: It defines the body's friction with other bodies
- Restitution: It defines the bounciness of the body

If restitution is less than 1, this means if you drop a ball it will bounce back, but the distance of each bounce will be less than previous bounce and the distance will keep decreasing until the object stops. If restitution is 1, this ball would bounce right back to the same position, fall again, and bounce again eternally. It will not lose its distance or speed, and if restitution is greater than 1, the speed and distance will increase.

The values I provide are similar to what was used in Mashballs, but you can experiment with them to achieve any desired effect.

```
local fixture = body:createFixture{shape = circle, density = 1.0,
    friction = 0.1, restitution = 0.5}
```

And as the last thing, we set the type of object just so we will know what type it is later, and do a little referencing by setting this body as an instance property of our `MainBall` class and also setting reference to this class on our body. So we could always get one from the other, no matter what world (Gideros or Box2D) we are in.

```
body.type = "main"
self.body = body
body.object = self
```

 If you are an experienced Box2D user, by this time you could be tempted to set scaling ratio and apply it to all values to optimize Box2D engine efficiency, but in Gideros this is done internally to all values and the default scale value is 30. But you can change it using the b2.setScale(scale) method, you need to do that only after requiring Box2D plugin, before creating world and any other Box2D object.

Now let's try out our `MainBall` class. Let's go to the `LevelScene:init()` method and create the instance of the `MainBall` class by passing reference to the `LevelScene` instance and some coordinates (100, 100), and save it as instance property of `LevelScene`.

Don't forget to add it to the scene too, so it would be rendered.

```
self.mainBall = MainBall.new(self, 400, 200)
self:addChild(self.mainBall)
```

When that's done, try running the project and press the **Start Game** button to go to `LevelScene`. We should see the graphic of our main ball and a transparent red circle around it, the debug draw.

As you see, the debug draw is slightly larger than our graphic and that is because we simply took half of the graphics width as the body's radius. But our graphic might not be a perfect circle (in our case it has hair). It also might contain some transparent areas around it. Thus, simply taking the width of image might not work all the time.

That is actually one of the reasons to use debug draw. We can now tweak the size of the body to match our image.

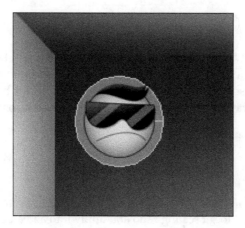

Now let's go to the line in the `MainBall:init()` method where we got our `radius` and make it a little smaller by multiplying with some tweaked value like `0.85`.

```
--get radius
local radius = (self.bitmap:getWidth()/2)*0.85
```

If you rerun the project, you should see that debug draw is just around the image, which is basically what we want.

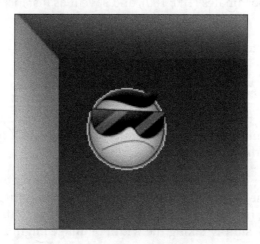

Running the world

Now as you should have noticed, while we were debugging the size of our body, the object and body are rendered, but they won't move.

That is because we also need to run our world step-by-step, literally. We need to call the world:step() method periodically to update the state of the physics world.

To do that we need to define the event handler, that will handle our ENTER_FRAME event. The ENTER_FRAME event is executed every time rendering frame is updated by the processor. So all the animation, moving things, and so on, are done inside this event. Running the physics world is no exception.

So let's define the simple LevelScene:onEnterFrame method to handle the ENTER_FRAME event in which we will update the state of our world. In this event handler, we first check if our game was paused and then call the self.world:step() method by providing the number of steps we should perform in the world.

```
function LevelScene:onEnterFrame()
  if not self.paused then
    -- update the world state
    self.world:step(1/60, 8, 3)
  end
end
```

Now let's add this event listener inside the LevelScene:init() method:

```
--run world
self:addEventListener(Event.ENTER_FRAME, self.onEnterFrame, self)
```

If we run the world now, we will see that our debug drawing is moving, but our Bitmap image is not following it. This is because we also need to update the Sprite object positions based on their body positions.

This means we will also need a place where to store all the Sprite objects which will have bodies attached to them, so we define it as empty self.bodies tables inside the LevelScene:init() method.

```
--store all bodies sprites here
self.bodies = {}
```

Next let's update the onEnterFrame event, so we would go through all the bodies and update their objects' positions accordingly.

For each body, we will update object position and the angle of its visual representation on the screen. Note that here we again convert the angle from radians to degrees, because of differences between Gideros and Box2D.

Note, we defined local body variable outside the loop. That is only due to efficiency, so we won't have to redefine this variable and allocate memory for it again on each cycle.

```
function LevelScene:onEnterFrame()
  if not self.paused then
    -- update the world state
    self.world:step(1/60, 8, 3)
    --iterate through all child sprites
    local body
    for i = 1, #self.bodies do
      --get specific body
      body = self.bodies[i]
      --update object's position to match box2d world object's
        position
      --apply coordinates to sprite
      body.object:setPosition(body:getPosition())
      --apply rotation to sprite
      body.object:setRotation(math.deg(body:getAngle()))
    end
  end
end
```

Then let's go back inside `MainBall.lua` and add our body to the scene's body table in the `init` method. This is important, because without adding body to the table, its position will not be updated inside the `LevelScene:onEnterFrame` event.

```
table.insert(self.level.bodies, body)
```

Now try and run the project, you will see that our image will move according to the debug drawing.

If we also try to press the menu button, one of two things might happen: the menu might open and it will be ok, or the main ball might start to fall without the menu opening. The difference of the results is in the order. The event in Gideros starts propagating from newly added elements to the older element, same as z index. So if we want the menu button to stop propagating the event before it reaches the main ball, we need to add a menu button to the scene, after we have added the main ball, at the end of the `LevelScene:init()` method.

Setting up world boundaries

It all seems to be running well. But hey! The ball just falls off the screen. That's why we need to set up the world boundaries.

Since it will not be an object we will interact with much in the game, but just a simple boundary, we will not create a separate class for it, but rather simply use `ChainShape` and create a simple rectangle terrain that surrounds our screen.

We don't even need any graphic to represent it (we already have boundaries drawn in our background graphic) and we won't have to update its position, because it will be a simple static body.

So let's create it inside the `LevelScene:init()` method. Same as before, we create a body, but now provide the `b2.STATIC_BODY` constant to indicate that we are creating static body and we set this body's position to the coordinates (0,0).

```
local body = self.world:createBody{type = b2.STATIC_BODY}
body:setPosition(0, 0)
```

Then we create a `ChainShape` object and provide screen dimensions to it. This process is similar to drawing with the `Shape` class.

```
local chain = b2.ChainShape.new()
chain:createLoop(
  0,0,
  conf.width, 0,
  conf.width, conf.height,
  0, conf.height
)
```

Finally, we create a fixture with the created shape and some physical properties.

```
local fixture = body:createFixture{shape = chain, density = 1.0,
    friction = 1, restitution = 0.5}
```

Now after running our project and going to the level scene, you will see that main ball drops on the ground and stays there.

Interaction with physical bodies

Now our ball simply drops to the ground, but what we want is to launch it as from a slingshot, like in the real Mashballs game.

Now with the simple `Sprite` objects, we would simply change their coordinates and so on, but we can't do that with the physical bodies, especially not with the dynamic ones, because we would only move the image, but the physical body would still be left in the previous position. In the best case, the image would be simply out back on the next `ENTER_FRAME` event in the worst case, which could break the whole physics emulation, resulting the image being in completely another position than the simulated physical body.

Instead, we may interact with dynamic objects in a physical way, by applying forces, impulses, torque, and by setting velocities of physical bodies.

Setting velocity is more like providing a constant speed to the body, until it gets opposed by other forces (like in collisions). Setting torque basically means making a body spin around its center.

While it is easy to explain the velocity and torque, the difference between force and impulse is not so big, even unnoticeable. They both apply momentum force to object, leaving only inertia, no continuous force like in case of setting velocity. But it is the way how they apply them what makes them different.

Firstly, impulse is applied instantly while force will start work only after `world:step` is called for the next time.

Secondly, impulse is not time dependent and is applied all completely, while force is applied only for a fraction of a second (between two `world:step` method calls). And to reach the same reaction as with linear impulse, you would need to apply it again on each step's call for a whole second.

Thirdly, as force is only applied by small time fractions, it is more influenced by other forces, such as gravity.

Therefore, in most cases, when you want to launch an object in some direction, you would use impulse and if you would want to apply specific force for some specific time period, you would use force.

So, in the original game, at first there is only a bitmap, users drag it and aim with it. After a user releases it, we need to create a physical body for our bitmap and apply impulse based on the direction and force our user has used to drag the image away from the start position.

Let's start by separating the body creation from the `MainBall:init()` method to a new method called `MainBall:createBody()`, which we could use later to create the body for our image.

```
function MainBall:createBody()
  --get radius
  local radius = (self.bitmap:getWidth()/2)*0.85

  --create box2d physical object
  local body = self.level.world:createBody{type = b2.DYNAMIC_BODY}

  --copy all state of object
  body:setPosition(self:getPosition())
  body:setAngle(math.rad(self:getRotation()))

  local circle = b2.CircleShape.new(0, 0, radius)

  local fixture = body:createFixture{shape = circle, density =
    1.0,
  friction = 0.1, restitution = 0.2}

  body.type = "main"
  self.body = body
  body.object = self

  table.insert(self.level.bodies, body)
end
```

Now let's create the `onMouseDown` method, an event handle for the `MOUSE_DOWN` event, when the user starts touching the main ball.

Inside it we don't need to check for `hitTestPoint` as we want the touch event to work on the whole screen. But what we need to do is to stop the propagation to other events, save our current coordinates as start position, and set a flag that our main ball is now being dragged.

```
function MainBall:onMouseDown(e)
  e:stopPropagation()
  self.startX = self:getX()
  self.startY = self:getY()
  self.isDragged = true
end
```

The next thing to handle is the MOUSE_MOVE event, so let's create the onMouseMove method.

First we check if our main ball is being dragged, by checking the isDragged flag, and if it is being dragged, let's stop further propagation of event. Then we want to limit the dragging radius of our main ball, thus let's set the radius r as 120 to limit dragging to 120 pixels radius.

We calculate the current vectors xVect and yVect based on start and current positions. Then we calculate the distance from the start position based on calculated vectors and store it in variable length.

After that, we can simply check if length is smaller or equal to allowed radius, we simply change our object's position to the mouse coordinates.

If the length is longer than the allowed radius, we need to calculate the coefficient by which we can multiply the vectors to get the vector which would be equal to our allowed radius. In other words, we set the object on the boundary coordinates of our radius by taking the user's provided direction into consideration.

```
function MainBall:onMouseMove(e)
  if self.isDragged  then
    e:stopPropagation()
    local r = 120
    local xVect = (e.x-self.startX)
    local yVect = (e.y-self.startY)
    local length = math.sqrt(xVect*xVect + yVect*yVect)

    if length <= r then
      self:setPosition(e.x, e.y)
    else
      local coef = math.sqrt((r*r)/(xVect*xVect+yVect*yVect))
      self:setX(self.startX+xVect*coef)
      self:setY(self.startY+yVect*coef)
    end
  end
end
```

The last thing to do is to handle the MOUSE_UP event using the onMouseUp method.

Inside that we similarly check if our main ball is being dragged and stop propagation of events if it is. Then we take off the flag of our object being dragged, well basically because the MOUSE_UP event means our object has been released.

It also means we can now create the physical body for our object by calling our previously created MainBall:createBody() method.

Next, we need to apply impulse based on the direction and distance from the starting point. We define the `strength` variable with value 10; we will use it to increase the vectors (you may change it if you want to launch objects with different relative strengths).

Then we calculate vectors again from the starting and current positions multiplied by the strength we just defined, and we apply the impulse with these vectors by calling the `self.body:applyLinearImpulse` method and providing vectors and hit coordinates as mass center (or simply current objects coordinates).

The last thing to do is to remove all mouse event listeners from our object, since we won't use them anymore until the next scene is loaded, when we will create a new main ball.

```
function MainBall:onMouseUp(e)
  if self.isDragged  then
    e:stopPropagation()
    self.isDragged = false
    self:createBody()
    --define strength of slingshot
    local strength = 10
    --calculate force vector based on strength
    --and distance of pull
    local xVect = (self.startX - self:getX())*strength
    local yVect = (self.startY - self:getY())*strength
    --applye impulse to target
    self.body:applyLinearImpulse(xVect, yVect, self:getX(),
      self:getY())

    self:removeEventListener(Event.MOUSE_DOWN, self.onMouseDown,
      self)
    self:removeEventListener(Event.MOUSE_MOVE, self.onMouseMove,
      self)
    self:removeEventListener(Event.MOUSE_UP, self.onMouseUp, self)
  end
end
```

Now launch the project, go to your level scene, and try dragging and releasing the main ball. It should behave similarly to what you saw in the real game.

Handling Box2D collisions

Now let's create another type of game element, called touch ball, which will represent the ball that the main ball needs to hit and we will know that by listening to collision events.

So first create a `TouchBall.lua` file inside the `objects` folder and define a `TouchBall` class in it which inherits from `Sprite`.

```
TouchBall = Core.class(Sprite)
```

Creating a `TouchBall` object will be quite similar to creating `MainBall`. It will accept same parameters and do completely the same stuff, only loading a different graphic and setting a different body type.

So at first we store reference to scene and set position of the object. Then we create a `Bitmap` object from graphic of the touch ball and set its anchor point to 0.5 and add this `Bitmap` object to the `TouchBall` class instance.

```
function TouchBall:init(level, x, y)
  self.level = level
  self:setPosition(x,y)

  --create bitmap object from ball graphic
  self.bitmap =
    Bitmap.new(self.level.g:getTextureRegion("touch4.png"))
  --reference center of the ball for positioning
  self.bitmap:setAnchorPoint(0.5,0.5)
  self:addChild(self.bitmap)
end
```

Then similarly, like in the `MainBall` class, we can define a `TouchBall:createBody()` method. We get the radius from half of the image width and multiply it by the tweaked ratio 0.85. Then we create a body, only now by passing the `b2.STATIC_BODY` value to create a static body. After that we copy the position and angle of the represented bitmap image.

Now we need to create a circle shape with the radius provided and create a fixture using this shape. And similarly, like we did with `MainBall`, we set up references to both the body and object, so we could use them in both worlds.

```
function TouchBall:createBody()
  --get radius
  local radius = (self.bitmap:getWidth()/2)*0.85

  --create box2d physical object
  local body = self.level.world:createBody{type = b2.STATIC_BODY}
```

```
--copy all state of object
body:setPosition(self:getPosition())
body:setAngle(math.rad(self:getRotation()))

local circle = b2.CircleShape.new(0, 0, radius)

local fixture = body:createFixture{shape = circle, density = 1,
friction = 0.1, restitution = 0.5}

body.type = "touch"
self.body = body
body.object = self
end
```

We don't need to add the `TouchBall` body to the bodies list using `table.insert(self.level.bodies, body)` because it is a static body and it won't move. But if we created a dynamic object, we would also have to include it in the bodies list.

 Since the code between the `MainBall` and `TouchBall` classes is quite similar, we could even create one abstract class `Ball`, and make both `MainBall` and `TouchBall` inherit from it, setting properties which are different to them inside their constructors and adding only new needed methods.

So let's go to the `LevelScene:init()` method and add this `TouchBall` to our level scene. We do it in similar way, by creating an instance of the `TouchBall` class and providing all required parameters and adding this instance to the scene.

```
local touch = TouchBall.new(self, 200, 100)
self:addChild(touch)
```

 You can create many different objects like this for your game, having a separate class representing each object and tweaking all the physical parameters internally.

Now if you run the project, you will see we also have the `TouchBall` object appearing on our level scene. As we have two different objects, let's listen to when they will collide and change the image of the main ball to a smile.

First let's set up the `MainBall:smile()` method inside the `MainBall.lua` file. To accomplish this, we will simply change the texture of the `MainBall` bitmap to some other, with the smile, and then change it back after 2 seconds (or 2000 milliseconds) using the `Timer.delayedCall` function, which will execute the provided function after a specified number of milliseconds.

```lua
function MainBall:smile()
  local smileTexture = self.level.g:getTextureRegion("main2.png")
  self.bitmap:setTextureRegion(smileTexture)
  Timer.delayedCall(2000, function()
    local normal = self.level.g:getTextureRegion("main1.png")
    self.bitmap:setTextureRegion(normal)
  end)
end
```

Then let's go to `LevelScene.lua` and create a new method for handling collisions, called the `LevelScene:onBeginContact ()` method. There, we will get the fixtures that collide from the event object. Then we can get the bodies of the fixtures. After that we need to determine which bodies are colliding.

First we check if both bodies have a property type defined, like we defined them in both the `MainBall` and `TouchBall` classes. If they are not defined for both bodies, the main ball is most probably colliding with the boundary wall, and we are not interested in this collision. But if we have defined types for both bodies, this collision should interest us.

After that we need to determine which bodies actually collide, which one is `main`, which is `touch`, and so on. Usually, you would have to go around and test for each possible variation, like check if `bodyA` is `main` and then check if `bodyB` is `main`, and so on.

```lua
if bodyA.type == "main" then
  local main = bodyA
elseif bodyB.type == "main"
  local main = bodyB
end
```

But here is the neat trick. Box2D places the first created body as `bodyA` and second created body as `bodyB`. So, if two bodies are colliding, the one that was created first will be `bodyA`.

Now if you remember, we create the body for the main ball only after we touch, drag, and release it. This means that all the elements on the scene must be loaded before. So we have a guarantee that if the main ball is colliding with any object, it will always be the `bodyB` value.

After we have determined if the collision is between the `touch` and `main` balls, we can call the `smile()` method on the `bodyB` object property, which as we remember is the reference to the `MainBall` class.

```
function LevelScene:onBeginContact(e)
   --getting contact bodies
   local fixtureA = e.fixtureA
   local fixtureB = e.fixtureB
   local bodyA = fixtureA:getBody()
   local bodyB = fixtureB:getBody()
   --check if this collision interests us
   if bodyA.type and bodyB.type then
     --check which bodies collide
     if bodyA.type == "touch" and bodyB.type == "main" then
       --smile
       bodyB.object:smile()
     end
   end
end
```

Now go to our level scene and try to hit the touch ball with our main ball and you will see the main ball will smile for 2 seconds after hitting the touch ball, which means we have successfully listened to a collision event and determined which bodies were actually colliding.

To make the collision count only the first hit, we can remove the touch type from the ball on collision, so we would know we already hit it and we are not interested in this object anymore and make the main ball smile only once per collision with each touch ball.

```
--smile
bodyB.object:smile()
bodyA.type = nil
```

Managing packs and levels

Now that we have finished the prototype of our game and see that it works, let's implement the pack and level logic, as well as player progression between levels.

This is the part where you take your game out of prototype state and gamify it with more engagement loops and sense of progression, and make it into something you could show to others. I usually start to bother my friends with trying the new game after implementing the simple tutorial level pack.

Defining packs

First let's create a simple file, where we would define our packs and the number of levels in them. So head to your Gideros Studio and add a `packs.lua` file to your project. Inside it we will define a simple packs table which would contain subtables, representing each pack with name of the pack, and the number of levels in it.

```lua
packs = {
  {
    name = "First pack",
    levels = 15
  },
  {
    name = "Second pack",
    levels = 15
  },
}
```

Now based on this definition, we can create a scene, where we can allow a user to switch between packs and select any level in the pack.

Creating LevelSelectScene

So create `LevelSelectScene.lua` inside the Gideros project `scenes` folder and define a `LevelSelectScene` class inherited from `Sprite` in it.

```lua
LevelSelectScene = Core.class(Sprite)
```

Now let's create the `init` method and put the usual stuff in it, the background graphic, the back button, and also code for handling Android back button, which in both cases will go back to the start scene.

```lua
function LevelSelectScene:init()
local bg = Bitmap.new(Texture.new("images/bg.jpg", true))
  bg:setAnchorPoint(0.5, 0.5)
```

```
    bg:setPosition(conf.width/2, conf.height/2)
    self:addChild(bg)

    local backText = TextField.new(conf.fontMedium, "Back")
    backText:setTextColor(0xffff00)
    local backButton = Button.new(backText)
    backButton:setPosition((conf.width - backButton:getWidth())/2,
      conf.height - 30)
    self:addChild(backButton)
    backButton:addEventListener("click", function()
      sceneManager:changeScene("start", conf.transitionTime,
        conf.transition, conf.easing)
    end)

    self:addEventListener(Event.KEY_DOWN, function(event)
      if event.keyCode == KeyCode.BACK then
        sceneManager:changeScene("start", conf.transitionTime,
          conf.transition, conf.easing)
      end
    end)
  end
```

As usual, we also need to add this scene to our `sceneManager` in the `main.lua` file.

```
--level select scene
["levelselect"] = LevelSelectScene,
```

Now as we have the `levelSelect` scene between `StartScene` and `LevelScene`, we need to chain them properly, so when pressing on the **Start Game** button we would go to the `levelselect` scene rather than the level scene.

So let's head to our `StartScene.lua` and change the scene of our `startButton` event handler to the `levelselect` scene.

```
startButton:addEventListener("click", function()
  sceneManager:changeScene("levelselect", conf.transitionTime,
    conf.transition, conf.easing)
end)
```

If you run the project now, and click on **Start Game**, you should be redirected to the `levelselect` scene, which would have a **Back** button; by clicking it you would go back to `StartScene`.

The next thing to do is to allow the user to select a level from a specific pack. Thus we need to know what the current selected pack is. It would also be cool to store the selected pack persistently, so when the user comes back to the game, he/she would see the last pack played on the level select screen. We have our `Settings` class for that purpose.

So open up your `Settings.lua` inside the `classes` folder and add a couple of new values to your initial settings table, `curPack` for current pack and `curLevel` for currently selected level, which we will need later too.

```
--our initial settings
local settings = {
  username = "Player",
  curPack = 1,
  curLevel = 1
}
```

Now, whenever a player opens the game, the default pack (and level) will be selected as 1. So let's head back to our `LevelSelectScene.lua` and draw up some levels for users to select.

As you might recall, we defined information about our packs inside `packs.lua`. So let's use it and display the name of the currently selected pack as heading.

First we need to retrieve the current pack from settings and set it as instance property of the `LevelSelectScene` class.

```
self.curPack = sets:get("curPack")
```

Then we can create `TextField` with our defined medium font and provide a pack name as text. We only need to set the color of the text, provide the position we want, and add it to the scene.

```
local packHeading = TextField.new(conf.fontMedium,
  packs[self.curPack].name)
packHeading:setTextColor(0xffff00)
packHeading:setPosition((conf.width - packHeading:getWidth())/2,
  50)
self:addChild(packHeading)
```

Generating a grid of levels

It is now time to generate our grid-like level selection, where our player can see how many levels are there in the pack, and the status of the levels, locked and unlocked. You can see an example of the resulting screen in the following screenshot:

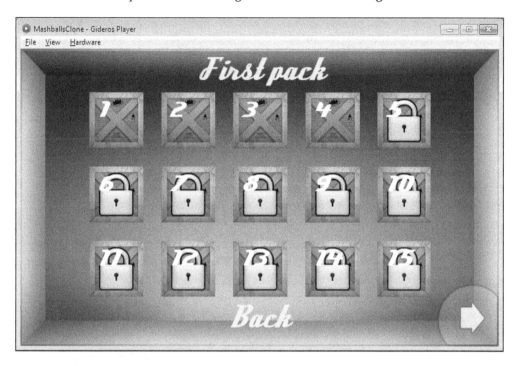

Now let's copy images we will be using for locked/unlocked levels to our project's `images` folder and add them in Gideros Studio too.

Then let's create a `Sprite` layer for our grid and add it to the scene.

```
local grid = Sprite.new()
self:addChild(grid)
```

After that we need to define some variable, such as current position where we are going to place the next level icon, the step to increase position with each icon, the padding between icons, the number of total columns in the row, and the current row we are handling.

```
local currentX, currentY = 0, 0 -- start coordinates
local step = 100 -- increase per level
local padding = 20 --padding between columns and rows
local totalCol = 5 -- total count of columns
local curCol = 0 --current column processing
```

Next we need to define the loop, to go from level 1 to the number of levels defined in
`packs.lua`.

```
for i = 1, packs[self.curPack].levels do

end
```

In this loop we need to create an image that will represent the level icon. For now
let's display all the levels as locked ones. We create a `Bitmap` object from the image
texture and set its position to `currentX` and `currentY` positions and add it to `grid`.

```
--create level image
local level = Bitmap.new(Texture.new("images/level_locked.png",
  true))
level:setPosition(currentX, currentY)
grid:addChild(level)
```

Next let's create `levelNumber` to display in the upper-left corner of the level icon. We
can take the current level number from the loop variable `i` and create a `TextField`
object with its value. Then we set its color and position in the upper-left corner and
add it to the level icon.

```
--add level number
local levelNumber = TextField.new(conf.fontMedium, i)
levelNumber:setTextColor(0xffffff)
levelNumber:setPosition(10, 40)
level:addChild(levelNumber)
```

As the last thing, we need to calculate the correct position where to place the
next level icon. So we increase the `curCol` counter and check if it has reached
the maximum of `totalCol` in the row. If yes, we reset the `curCol` and `currentX`
positions and increment the `currentY` position to go to the next row, and if not, we
simply increase the `currentX` position to go to the next level icon in the row.

```
--manipulate level position in the grid
curCol = curCol + 1
if curCol == totalCol then
  curCol = 0
  currentX = 0
  currentY = currentY + padding + step
else
  currentX = currentX + padding + step
end
```

As a result, we have a grid of levels to select from our current pack.

Switching between packs

But how can we change a pack? Let's add the right and left button images to select packs. First copy the images to your project's `images` folder and add them inside Gideros Studio in the `images` folder.

So how could we actually switch the pack on the same scene? Well, since we got our current pack from the settings, it would make sense if we simply changed `curPack` inside settings and went straight back to this same scene. Let me show you how.

First let's define the `LevelSelectScene:nextPack()` method. Inside it we will check whether `self.curPack` is not the last pack. We can do that by checking the number of packs inside the packs table and if it's greater than the number of the current pack, we save `self.curPack + 1` to the `Settings` class and reset this scene. So next time this scene will load, it will retrieve the newly set `self.curPack` number and load its name and levels instead.

An additional thing to note is that, for the more interesting transition, we selected the `SceneManager.moveFromRight` transition, because we want the new pack to come from the right side.

```
function LevelSelectScene:nextPack()
  if self.curPack < #packs then
    sets:set("curPack", self.curPack + 1)
    sceneManager:changeScene("levelselect", conf.transitionTime,
      SceneManager.moveFromRight, conf.easing)
  end
end
```

Let's create a very similar `LevelSelectScene:prevPack()` method to switch to the previous pack. In the similar way, we check if `self.curPack` is not the first pack, and if it's not, we decrease current pack by one and save to the settings, and again reset this scene.

```
function LevelSelectScene:prevPack()
  if self.curPack > 1 then
    sets:set("curPack", self.curPack - 1)
    sceneManager:changeScene("levelselect", conf.transitionTime,
      SceneManager.moveFromLeft, conf.easing)
  end
end
```

As we used a combination of scene transitions as `SceneManager.moveFromRight` for the next pack and `SceneManager.moveFromLeft` for the previous pack, we will have a nice effect for switching between packs.

Now let's implement buttons to try and switch the pack. Go to the `LevelSelectScene:init()` method and let's add the button to switch to next pack. Again, we don't need this button if it is the last scene, so let's check if it is not the last scene, then simply create a `Bitmap` object with a right-arrow image and create a button from these `Bitmap` objects.

Next we set position with absolute offsets `conf.dx` and `conf.dy` to make it stick to the bottom-right corner. Then we simply add it to the scene and add the `nextPack()` method as event handler for the click event.

```
if self.curPack < #packs then
  local right = Bitmap.new(Texture.new("images/right.png", true))
  local rightButton = Button.new(right)
  rightButton:setPosition(conf.dx + conf.width -
    rightButton:getWidth(), conf.dy + conf.height -
    rightButton:getHeight())
  self:addChild(rightButton)
  rightButton:addEventListener("click", self.nextPack, self)
end
```

Let's add the previous pack button in very similar manner. Check if it is not the first pack. Then create the `Bitmap` object from the left-arrow image and create a button from it. Place the button in the bottom-left corner and add it to the scene. In the end, add the `prevPack()` method as event listener for the click event of our button.

```
if self.curPack > 1 then
  local left = Bitmap.new(Texture.new("images/left.png", true))
  local leftButton = Button.new(left)
  leftButton:setPosition(-conf.dx, conf.dy + conf.height -
    leftButton:getHeight())
  self:addChild(leftButton)
  leftButton:addEventListener("click", self.prevPack, self)
end
```

That's it, check it out by running the project and clicking on **Start Game**, you should see a great transition effect when switching between packs.

Creating the GameManager class

Next we need to manage our levels. We need to be able to check which are locked and which can be accessed by users. To do that, we will create a `GameManager` class, which will persistently store information about levels, was it unlocked and what score the user reached in this level, and when the user did it.

So let's create a new file called `GameManager.lua` inside our `classes` folder and create a class named `GameManager` inside it.

```
GameManager = Core.class()
```

Then we define the `init` method for the `GameManager` class and create an empty table in the `self.packs` property.

```
function GameManager:init()
  self.packs = {}
end
```

After that we need a method to load information about the previously saved pack. As we will be reading it every time we visit the `levelselect` scene, let's create smaller files representing each pack separately, rather than storing all in one single file.

Thus we will provide a pack number to the `loadPack()` method. We will check if we don't yet have any information on this pack, we need to load it using `dataSaver` and provide path to the `Documents` directory to save files, the same way we discussed in the previous chapter while implementing the `Settings` class. After loading, we should check again and if there is still no information about this pack, we simply create an empty table.

```
function GameManager:loadPack(pack)
  if self.packs[pack] == nil then
    self.packs[pack] = dataSaver.load("|D|scores"..pack)
  end
  if self.packs[pack] == nil then
    self.packs[pack] = {}
  end
end
```

Next, let's define a simple method to save specific packs. Again, we simply pass pack number and `dataSaver` saves whatever information we have stored for that pack.

```
function GameManager:save(pack)
  dataSaver.save("|D|scores"..pack, self.packs[pack])
end
```

The next method will create information about a new level, which had no information before. Here we simply create a new table for that specific level in that specific pack and we can set any initial values we want to track, and then provide setters and getters for each value. In the end we simply save the information about this pack.

```
function GameManager:createLevel(pack, level)
   self.packs[pack][level] = {}
   self.packs[pack][level].score = 0
   self.packs[pack][level].time = nil
   self.packs[pack][level].unlocked = false
   self:save(pack)
end
```

Now that we have all the helper methods, let's create a method which will check if the level is unlocked or not. So we will provide pack and level number to this method. It will first try to load the information it has about this pack, then if there is no information about this specific level stored, we will simply create information about the new level. After that we simply check if the level is unlocked or not by checking one of its properties, named unlocked.

```
function GameManager:isUnlocked(pack, level)
   self:loadPack(pack)
   if(self.packs[pack][level] == nil) then
     self:createLevel(pack, level)
   end
   return self.packs[pack][level].unlocked
end
```

We also need a method to unlock specific level. Again, we will provide pack and level number as parameters. Then we will try to load information about the pack and create this level if it does not exist yet. Then we check if this level is not yet unlocked, set its unlocked flag to true, and save this pack.

```
function GameManager:unlockLevel(pack, level)
   self:loadPack(pack)
   if(self.packs[pack][level] == nil) then
     self:createLevel(pack, level)
   end
   if not self.packs[pack][level].unlocked then
     self.packs[pack][level].unlocked = true
     self:save(pack)
   end
end
```

Here comes the most interesting method, which will automatically get the next level. It also needs to be able to get the first level of the next pack, if the current level was the last level of current pack. Additionally, we can make it to unlock the next level.

This method will take the current pack and level numbers, as well as the parameter unlock, which should indicate if we need to unlock the next level.

Now as usual, let's load the information about the pack. Then we try to increase the level number and check if the increased level number is higher than the total number of levels in this pack (the value of which can be known from `packs.lua`), then we set level as the first and increase the pack number.

As the last thing, we check if the new pack and level values are available in the `packs.lua` file. If yes, we simply unlock this level if we need to and return pack and level number, but if it's not available in the `packs.lua` file, it would mean we have exceeded defined packs and reached the end of the game, so we will simply return nil values.

```
function GameManager:getNextLevel(pack, level, unlock)
  self:loadPack(pack)
  level = level + 1
  if packs[pack].levels < level then
    level = 1
    pack = pack + 1
  end
  if packs[pack] and packs[pack].levels >= level then
    if unlock then
      self:unlockLevel(pack, level)
    end
    return pack, level
  else
    return nil, nil
  end
end
```

Implementing unlocked levels logic

Now when we have our GameManager class, let's use it in our levelselect scene. There are two ways you can do it here, either by creating a global GameManager class instance inside main.lua and use it throughout the project, or by creating a local instance inside specific scenes and use them when needed. As a guideline, if there is a large amount of packs and there are lots of levels in each pack, you should create local instance for each specific scene.

In case of global object, it would mean you will be keeping information about all loaded levels inside your memory. But on the other hand, you would not have to reload information about each level, and that can improve the loading time. So it is up to you, what you would sacrifice better.

But in reality, the information stored per level is quite less and it is more handy to have a single global reference than creating new objects every time it is needed.

So go to main.lua and create a global instance of the GameManager class.

```
gm = GameManager.new()
```

Then go to levelselectScene.lua, and inside the init method is to unlock the first level of the first pack, as we want the user to start playing with it. So we check, if the current pack is the first pack, and if the first level is not unlocked, we unlock it.

```
if self.curPack == 1 and not gm:isUnlocked(1, 1) then
   gm:unlockLevel(1, 1)
end
```

Then, inside our loop which creates a grid, we need to check for each level if it is locked, we leave it as it is; but if it is unlocked, we provide it a different image by creating our own Button with the other Bitmap image, saving the current level ID as the property of our instance and adding an event handler, to which we will pass the instance of our button as the first parameter. Inside the event handler, we simply set curLevel in our settings to the value of the provided ID and go to the level scene.

```
--create level image
local level
if gm:isUnlocked(self.curPack, i) then
   local bitmap =
     Bitmap.new(Texture.new("images/level_unlocked.png", true))
   level = Button.new(bitmap)
   level.id = i
   level:addEventListener("click", function(self)
     sets:set("curLevel", self.id)
     sceneManager:changeScene("level", conf.transitionTime,
       conf.transition, conf.easing)
   end, level)
else
   level = Bitmap.new(Texture.new("images/level_locked.png", true))
end
level:setPosition(currentX, currentY)
grid:addChild(level)
```

Now inside the `LevelScene:init()` method, we can read both `curPack` and `curLevel` values from the settings class to determine which level the user wants to load now. So let's go to `LevelScene.lua` and modify its `init` method to store current pack and level information as instance properties.

```
self.curPack = sets:get("curPack")
self.curLevel = sets:get("curLevel")
```

Reading level definitions

The next thing for us to do is to create a level definition file for each level. Then read it inside `level.lua` based on what level we currently want to load, and place all the objects according to the level definition.

The level definition format may depend on what you are using to create your levels. You may use some third-party software, which will generate you the definition automatically and you would only have to interpret it in Gideros.

In our case, as the example levels will contain small number of objects, we will even be able to edit it by hand in any text editor without much confusion. The level definition will be a simple JSON file with object names and coordinates. So let's create a `levels` folder inside Gideros Studio and add a simple level definition `1-1.json` (first number indicating pack, second number indicating level). In this level definition, we would define type of object (main or touch) and its position on the level (x and y coordinates).

```
[{"type":"main","x":400,"y":150},
 {"type":"touch","x":400,"y":400}]
```

Additionally, you could define the dimensions, rotation, and other properties in your level definitions and interpret them all inside your Gideros project.

Let's add a couple of more levels, just to test the functionality. So create `1-2.json` with some more main and touch balls.

```
[{"type":"main","x":400,"y":150},{"type":"touch","x":250,"y":400},
 {"type":"touch","x":525,"y":400}]
```

Let's also create a third level `1-3.json` with differently positioned touch balls.

```
[{"type":"main","x":400,"y":150},{"type":"touch","x":250,"y":225},
 {"type":"touch","x":600,"y":60}]
```

Now let's add these definitions to the `levels` folder inside Gideros Studio and try to read it in the `levels.lua` file's `LevelScene:init()` method.

First we remove the code where we simply create the `MainBall` and `TouchBall` test objects, and instead we load the level definition, based on the `curPack` and `curLevel` settings. Then we create an instance property `self.ballsLeft` where we will store how many balls are left to hit.

```
self.curPack = sets:get("curPack")
self.curLevel = sets:get("curLevel")

self.level = dataSaver.load("levels/"..self.curPack.."-
   "..self.curLevel)
self.ballsLeft = 0
```

Then we loop through all objects defined in level definition and create these objects in our game. If it is a main type, we create `MainBall` with the specified coordinates. The same goes for `TouchBall`, only we additionally count how many `TouchBalls` there are in the game.

```
for i, value in ipairs(self.level) do
  if value.type == "main" then
    self.mainBall = MainBall.new(self, value.x, value.y)
    self:addChild(self.mainBall)
  elseif value.type == "touch" then
    local touch = TouchBall.new(self,  value.x, value.y)
    self:addChild(touch)
    self.ballsLeft = self.ballsLeft + 1
  end
end
```

Completing the level

Now let's create a method `LevelScene:completed()` where we would unlock the next level and present some dialog to move users to this newly unlocked level.

In the `LevelScene:completed()` method, we will try to get the next level from `GameManager`. If the next level or pack is nil, it means we reached the end of the game, thus we will display the message accordingly and go to `StartScene`.

If there is a next level, we will store it in the `Settings` class, so we could retrieve it on the next level load, then display the respective message and go to the same level scene, which will load level definition of the level and pack number stored in the `Settings` class.

Upon completion, we will display the `AlertDialog` object, which in Gideros represents simple native dialog with a message; the way it looks depends on the platform it is used on.

```
function LevelScene:completed()
  self.curPack, self.curLevel = gm:getNextLevel(self.curPack,
    self.curLevel, true)
  --if curPack is nil it means we reached the end of the game
  if self.curPack == nil then
    local dialog = AlertDialog.new("Game Completed", "You have
      completed the game", "Yay")
    dialog:addEventListener(Event.COMPLETE, function()
      --goto main sceneManager
      sceneManager:changeScene("start", conf.transitionTime,
        conf.transition, conf.easing)
    end)
    dialog:show()
  else
    -- we will store new pack and level ids in settings
    sets:set("curPack", self.curPack)
    sets:set("curLevel", self.curLevel)

    local dialog = AlertDialog.new("Level Completed", "Continue to
      next Level", "OK")
    dialog:addEventListener(Event.COMPLETE, function()
      sceneManager:changeScene("level", conf.transitionTime,
        conf.transition, conf.easing)
    end)
    dialog:show()
  end
end
```

Now we need to only determine when the level will complete. That is why we created the `self.ballsLeft` property, so we could subtract from it every time we hit new touch ball, and if it reached zero, we would know that we have completed the level. So let's add it to the collision event handler.

```
--smile
bodyB.object:smile()
bodyA.type = nil
self.ballsLeft = self.ballsLeft - 1
if self.ballsLeft == 0 then
  self:completed()
end
```

And that's it, we can define any number of levels we want to, just don't forget to update `packs.lua` accordingly.

Summary

Now we have implemented our main game logic and we can define multiple packs and levels, as also create, read, and interpret level definitions and create different game objects as separate Gideros classes. Additionally, we can manage unlocking levels upon completion of the previous level.

In the next chapter, we will make our game more advanced and polished by adding animations and sound effects, and also by changing how we interact with the game and its controls, and making the game more engaging by adding scores.

4

Polishing the Game

Now that we have the basics covered and have a working prototype of our game, let's improve it a bit by adding some of the most common enhancements to both the look and feel of our game and its gameplay.

This chapter will describe how to spice up our game to make it more appealing and alive. Topics covered in this chapter are:

- Adding background music and sound effects to the game
- Using high scores for **gamification**
- Animating game elements
- Tweening to make the game more dynamic
- Improving gameplay by adding gestures
- Providing ways to players to interact with game elements

Adding sounds

Although usually underrated by developers, background music and sound effects are an important part of any game. It sets up the mood and compliments the gameplay. But that's aesthetics. What we need to learn is how to set up background music and sound effects in Gideros.

Gideros API for playing sounds is pretty straightforward. First, we load sound by creating the `Sound` class instance.

```
local sound = Sound.new("mysound.mp3")
```

And then we play this sound by calling the `sound:play()` method.

In Gideros, a good practice is to use MP3 format for background music or sounds that do not require immediate play. This is because MP3 is a compressed format and more resources would be required to uncompress it.

For sound effects and other sounds that do require immediate play, you should use WAV files, because this file format is uncompressed and can be read and played immediately.

But what we need to do is to provide the ability to turn the sounds off and on as well. So what we will do here is create two separate classes, one for background music and other for sound effects, and provide the player with the option to enable/disable them inside the **Options** screen.

Adding background music

First let's create a `Music` class, which will deal with the playing of the background music. Let's create a `Music.lua` file inside the `classes` folder in Gideros Studio.

As music is not something we will add to the stage that will be rendered, we don't need to inherit this class from `sprite`. But we will want to dispatch events when music is turned on or off, thus we need to inherit from the `EventDispatcher` class.

```
Music = Core.class(EventDispatcher)
```

Then, inside the `init` method, we will retrieve the path to the music file and create a `Sound` object from it. We will also prepare events, which will be dispatched when sound is turned on or off.

```
function Music:init(music)
   --load main theme
   self.theme = Sound.new(music)
   self.eventOn = Event.new("musicOn")
   self.eventOff = Event.new("musicOff")
end
```

After this, let's create a `Music:on()` method which will start playing the sound from the start, and pass `true` to indicate that we need infinite looping of this sound. Additionally, we dispatch the `musicOn` event.

```
--turn music on
function Music:on()
   if not self.channel then
      self.channel = self.theme:play(0, true)
      self:dispatchEvent(self.eventOn)
   end
end
```

Now quite similarly, to turn the music off, we will create a `Music:off()` method, which will stop playing the music channel and nil it out. So, it frees memory and dispatches the `musicOff` event as well.

```
--turn music off
function Music:off()
  if self.channel then
    self.channel:stop()
    self.channel = nil
    self:dispatchEvent(self.eventOff)
  end
end
```

Now let's try out our class. First let's create a `sounds` folder in our project folder and in the Gideros Studio. Then we can copy all the sounds that we will be using to this folder and add them to the Gideros Studio.

Now, we also need a setting which will be saved persistently to indicate if music is currently on or off. To implement this, we will go to the `Settings.lua` file and add `music = true` to the initial settings table.

```
--our initial settings
local settings = {
  username = "Player",
  curPack = 1,
  curLevel = 1,
  music = true
}
```

Now let's go to our `main.lua` file and create an instance of our `Music` class by providing the path to the background music file.

```
--background music
music = Music.new("sounds/main.mp3")
```

Then we need to add events to listen when music is turned on or off, and update our settings accordingly. If the `musicOn` event is dispatched, we set the `music` setting to `true`; if the `musicOff` event is dispatched, we set the `music` setting to `false`. The third value, `true`, indicates that we want to save this setting immediately.

```
--when music gets enabled
music:addEventListener("musicOn", function()
  sets:set("music", true, true)
end)
--when music gets disabled
```

```
music:addEventListener("musicOff", function()
   sets:set("music", false, true)
end)
```

We also need to check what the current `music` setting is; if it is `true` we need to start playing the background music.

```
--play music if enabled
if sets:get("music") then
   music:on()
end
```

Now if you launch the project, you should hear the background music playing.

The last thing we need to do is provide an option to turn the music on/off. So let's go to `OptionsScene.lua` and add an option to switch the music. First, we create a text to indicate this is a music option. We set the text, its color, and position and add it to the scene.

```
local musicText = TextField.new(conf.fontSmall, "Music: ")
musicText:setPosition(100, 250)
musicText:setTextColor(0xffff00)
self:addChild(musicText)
```

Then, based on the music setting, we need to determine the text of the button. If the music is on, we will set the **Turn off** text; but if the music is off, we will set the **Turn on** text.

```
local switchText = "Turn on"
if sets:get("music") then
   switchText = "Turn off"
end
```

Then, we create the `TextField` object with this text and set its color.

```
local musicSwitch = TextField.new(conf.fontSmall, switchText)
musicSwitch:setTextColor(0x00ff00)
```

After that we can create a `Button` object from this text, position it, and add it to the scene.

```
local musicButton = Button.new(musicSwitch)
musicButton:setPosition(conf.width - musicButton:getWidth() - 100,
   250)
self:addChild(musicButton)
```

Now on the button-click event, we need to both toggle the music (on or off, based on the setting) and change the text of the button accordingly.

```
musicButton:addEventListener("click", function()
  if sets:get("music") then
    music:off()
    musicSwitch:setText("Turn on")
  else
    music:on()
    musicSwitch:setText("Turn off")
  end
end)
```

Try it out, launch the project and go to the **Options** screen. There you can turn the music on and off now.

Adding sound effects

Now similar to the background music, we will also create a class for sound effects called Sounds. The difference here is that we may need to play different sounds for different effects. For example, one for when touch ball is hit, another when the level is completed. Additionally, we won't play the same hit sound on every instance of a hit; but we could set multiple hit sounds and play a random hit sound on each occasion.

Another difference is that we need to know beforehand if we should play the sound effect or not. So, we will have an internal class flag to check if sounds are enabled.

Now let's create Sounds.lua inside the classes folder and create a Sounds class in it, which will inherit from EventDispatcher.

```
Sounds = Core.class(EventDispatcher)
```

In the Sounds:init() method, we define a self.isOn flag to check if sound is on or not and define a self.sounds table to store all the sound effects. Similar to the Music class, we will also define the soundsOn and soundsOff events.

```
function Sounds:init()
  self.isOn = false
  self.sounds = {}
  self.eventOn = Event.new("soundsOn")
  self.eventOff = Event.new("soundsOff")
end
```

Then quite similar to the Music class, we define on and off methods, which will first check the internal flag and then if needed toggle it, and dispatch the according event.

```
--turn sounds on
function Sounds:on()
   if not self.isOn then
     self.isOn = true
     self:dispatchEvent(self.eventOn)
   end
end



--turn sounds off
function Sounds:off()
   if self.isOn then
     self.isOn = false
     self:dispatchEvent(self.eventOff)
   end
end
```

The next method we need is for adding a specific sound to a specific sound effect name. So, the add method will accept sound effect name and a path to the sound file, then check if there is already a table for the specified sound effect and if not, create one. In the end we simply create a Sound object and add it to the table of the specific sound effect.

```
function Sounds:add(name, sound)
   if self.sounds[name] == nil then
     self.sounds[name] = {}
   end
   self.sounds[name][#self.sounds[name]+1] = Sound.new(sound)
end
```

The last method we will need is for playing the specific sound effect. In this method we check if the internal flag is on and whether we are allowed to play the sound. Then, we check if there are any sounds defined for this sound effect; if both are true, we simply play a random file for the specified sound effect. If there will be only one sound file defined for the specific sound effect, it will be played.

```
function Sounds:play(name)
   if self.isOn and self.sounds[name] then
     self.sounds[name][math.random(1, #self.sounds[name])]:play()
   end
end
```

Now, again we add the `sounds` setting as `true` inside our initial setting table in the `Settings` class.

```
sounds = true
```

Create the `Sounds` instance inside `main.lua` and bind events to update the settings, just like we did with the `Music` class.

```
--sounds
sounds = Sounds.new()
--set up sound events
--when sounds turn on
sounds:addEventListener("soundsOn", function()
  sets:set("sounds", true, true)
end)
--when sounds turn off
sounds:addEventListener("soundsOff", function()
  sets:set("sounds", false, true)
end)
```

After that we want to enable the sounds if the `sounds` setting value is `true`.

```
--enable sounds if setting enabled
if sets:get("sounds") then
  sounds:on()
end
```

Then, we need to add the sound files to the specific sound effects.

So in this example we will have two sound effects:

- `complete`: Sound effect with single sound file when level completes
- `hit`: Sound effect with multiple sounds when main ball hits touch ball

We can add them simply by calling our defined `add` method and pass the name of sound effect and the path to the file.

```
sounds:add("complete", "sounds/complete.wav")
sounds:add("hit", "sounds/hit0.wav")
sounds:add("hit", "sounds/hit1.wav")
sounds:add("hit", "sounds/hit2.wav")
sounds:add("hit", "sounds/hit3.wav")
```

Now let's go to `levelScene` and play the sound effects. First let's play the `complete` sound effect inside the `LevelScene:completed()` method.

```
sounds:play("complete")
```

Next, we will play the random hit sound inside the `onBeginContact` method when main ball hits touch ball.

```
sounds:play("hit")
```

Lastly, we want to add an option to enable the sound effects exactly the same way we did with background music.

We do so by creating a text to specify that it is a `sounds` option, setting its color and position, and adding it to the scene.

```
local soundsText = TextField.new(conf.fontSmall, "Sounds: ")
soundsText:setPosition(100, 300)
soundsText:setTextColor(0xffff00)
self:addChild(soundsText)
```

Then we create a `Button` object from the `TextField` object with the proper text—depending on sounds setting—and position it accordingly. Then we add it to the scene.

```
local switchText = "Turn on"
if sets:get("sounds") then
  switchText = "Turn off"
end
local soundsSwitch = TextField.new(conf.fontSmall, switchText)
soundsSwitch:setTextColor(0x00ff00)
local soundsButton = Button.new(soundsSwitch)
soundsButton:setPosition(conf.width - soundsButton:getWidth() -
  100, 300)
self:addChild(soundsButton)
```

Then adding the `click` event to `soundsButton`, to turn the sounds on and off and change button text accordingly.

```
soundsButton:addEventListener("click", function()
  if sets:get("sounds") then
    sounds:off()
    soundsSwitch:setText("Turn on")
  else
    sounds:on()
    soundsSwitch:setText("Turn off")
  end
end)
```

That's it. Now, we can add sounds to our game for the background music or in-game sound effects, and also provide an option for the player to turn the sounds on or off.

Adding high scores

Implementing high scores is a must for almost every game to make players compete with each other or to make players replay levels to improve their result. So let's modify our GameManager class to also manage score for each level.

Inside our GameManager class createLevel method, we already stored default score and time values, so now we only need methods to set and retrieve them.

First, we will create a method to set the score, which would simply take pack and level number and the user score as the parameters, and return true to indicate that the user has beat a high score or false if the user'sscore is lower than the highest score.

So, as done previously for almost each GameManager method, at first we try to load the pack and create the level information if we need. Then we check if the user's high score is higher than the saved one; and if it is, we save the new score and time when it was achieved. Then we return true, else we simply return false.

```
function GameManager:setScore(pack, level, score)
  self:loadPack(pack)
  if(self.packs[pack][level] == nil) then
    self:createLevel(pack, level)
  end
  if(self.packs[pack][level].score < score)then
    self.packs[pack][level].score = score
    self.packs[pack][level].time = os.time()
    self:save(pack)
    return true
  end
  return false
end
```

Now we can set the high score, but we also need a method to get the current high score for the specific level. We will take pack number and level as parameters, load the pack information, and create level information as needed. Then we can simply return the score and the time when the score was achieved.

```
function GameManager:getScore(pack, level)
  self:loadPack(pack)
  if(self.packs[pack][level] == nil) then
```

```
        self:createLevel(pack, level)
    end
    return self.packs[pack][level].score,
        self.packs[pack][level].time
end
```

In a similar manner, you can implement any additional level parameters, such as the time it took to complete level or with how many "stars" the level was completed. For each of these parameters included in the initial level information inside the `GameManager:createLevel` method, you would have to create its own getter and setter.

Now let's go to the `LevelScene` and implement score system in our game. First, inside the `LevelScene:init()` method, we will display the high score retrieved from the `GameManager` class.

Retrieving high scores

So, first we need to retrieve the high score and store it in the `highScore` variable. Then we create a `TextField` object with small font that will display our high score. We set text color and position, and then add it to the scene.

```
local highScore = gm:getScore(self.curPack, self.curLevel)
local highScoreText = TextField.new(conf.fontSmall, "Highscore:
"..highScore)
highScoreText:setTextColor(0xffff00)
highScoreText:setPosition(10, 25)
self:addChild(highScoreText)
```

Now let's do the same for the current score, which will be 0 at the start of the game. Unlike the high score which we will display and then forget about, we will make current score a `TextField` object as an instance property so that we can update the score later on.

Thus, we create a `self.score` variable where we can store the current score and a `self.scoreText` variable where we can store reference to the `TextField` object, which displays the score. Similar to the high score, we set its text color and position and add it to the scene.

```
self.score = 0
self.scoreText = TextField.new(conf.fontSmall, "Score: 0")
self.scoreText:setTextColor(0xffff00)
self.scoreText:setPosition(10, 55)
self:addChild(self.scoreText)
```

Updating high score on the screen

Now we need to create a method to update the score on the screen. Let's call it updateScore and pass the score points to this method and inside it; we will add these score points to the current score and update the self.scoreText object to display it on the screen.

```
function LevelScene:updateScore(score)
  self.score = self.score + score
  self.scoreText:setText("Score: "..self.score)
end
```

In this game our score will depend on how hard we hit touch ball. We already have the BEGIN_CONTACT event; but unfortunately when contact begins, we don't know yet what was the collision force. For this, we will have to add a new event to our Box2D world called POST_SOLVE.

So let's create the method onPostSolve first to handle this event. Quite similar to what we did with the onBeginContact method, we will retrieve the fixtures that collide and get their bodies. Then, we try to determine if bodies have type properties defined and whether they are the ones that can interest us.

```
function LevelScene:onPostSolve(e)
  --getting contact bodies
  local fixtureA = e.fixtureA
  local fixtureB = e.fixtureB
  local bodyA = fixtureA:getBody()
  local bodyB = fixtureB:getBody()
  --check if this collision interests us
  if bodyA.type and bodyB.type then
    --check which bodies collide
    if bodyA.type == "touch" and bodyB.type == "main" then
      --handle score here
    end
  end
end
```

The onPostSolve event will be called after the onBeginContact event; but as you might remember, we nil the type of TouchBall object on collision inside the onBeginContact instant. So in this state, we will never go inside the if bodyA.type == "touch" and bodyB.type == "main" then statement. Thus, we will need to remove the part of the code, which sets nil value and handles completion of the level from onBeginContact and move it to the onPostSolve method.

So now, we nil the type of `TouchBall` object in the `onPostSolve` method and update the score by getting the rounded value of the `maxImpulse` property from the event object. Then we determine if the game has ended by subtracting `self.ballsLeft` and checking if it has reached 0, just like we did in the `onBeginContact` method before.

```
bodyA.type = nil
self:updateScore(math.floor(e.maxImpulse))
self.ballsLeft = self.ballsLeft - 1
if self.ballsLeft == 0 then
  self:completed()
end
```

Now the last thing to do is to try to store the new score inside the `LevelScene:complete()` method. We will simply add one new line to call the `GameManager:setScore` method and pass the current pack, level, and the score that was saved in the `self.score` property.

```
local isNewHighScore = gm:setScore(self.curPack, self.curLevel,
  self.score)
```

Additionally, we retrieve a boolean value which will tell us if the user's score is the new high score, so that we know whether or not to update the message.

Now you can try to run the game and play couple of levels, then when you get back to those levels, you will see your high score saved and displayed. Can you beat your high score now and achieve a new one?

Creating animated game elements

Animations are a vital part of improving a game. They make your game look more polished and alive, which appeals to many players out there and that is why animation is one of the ways in which we will improve our game.

There are two main ways to animate elements in Gideros:

- Using frame animations and MovieClip class
- Tweening the properties of object using GTween class

Frame animations using MovieClip

First let's create a frame animation for our `TouchBall`. To create a `MovieClip` instance we need to pass the definition of the frames which will appear in animation.

Each row of animation contains information, such as, {1, 10, sprite}, which contains position number of start frame, position number of end frame, and the sprite inherited object that will be displayed during this span of frames (from start frame to end frame).

If you want to display the next sprite object without overlapping with previous one, we add another definition to the table by using the same start frame number as the previous sprite's end frame number plus one, {11, 20, sprite2}.

As we are running our game at 60 frames per second, if we would like a single sprite to appear for 1 second on the screen, we need to provide a frame span of 60 frames for it. So adding another row in table with sprite object which would appear for 1 second on the screen would look like this: {21, 80, sprite3}. Additionally, we could also tween these frames by providing start and end properties; but we don't need it now.

Now let's create our first frame animation. Open the TouchBall.lua file and then load the images we will be using in our animation. We have these images defined in our texture pack, which are named as touch0.png, touch1.png, and up to touch18.png. This was done intentionally so that we could load them in a loop.

First we define a frames table where we store the images for frames. Then, we create a Bitmap object for each texture and set its anchor point to 0.5 inside the loop from 0 to 18 (as our image names). After this, we simply store the reference of the Bitmap object into our frames table under the same ID that was used in the image.

```
local frames = {}
for i = 0, 18 do
  local bitmap = Bitmap.new(self.level.g:getTextureRegion("touch"..i.
.".png"))
  bitmap:setAnchorPoint(0.5, 0.5)
  frames[i] = bitmap
end
```

Now instead of creating a single Bitmap image to represent touch ball, we can create our MovieClip object by defining animations with loaded images. As discussed before, we provide the frame span in which each image will appear on the screen and provide this table to the MovieClip.new() method.

Some of the images will repeat. For example, to turn the head to each side multiple times, we just repeat the same images with new frame intervals.

```
self.bitmap = MovieClip.new{
  {1, 10, frames[0]},
  {11, 15, frames[1]},
  {16, 20, frames[2]},
```

```
    {21,  30,  frames[3] },
    {31,  40,  frames[4] },
    {41,  45,  frames[5] },
    {46,  50,  frames[4] },
    {51,  55,  frames[6] },
    {56,  60,  frames[4] },
    {61,  65,  frames[5] },
    {66,  70,  frames[4] },
    {71,  75,  frames[6] },
    {76,  80,  frames[4] },
    {81,  85,  frames[5] },
    {86,  90,  frames[4] },
    {91,  95,  frames[6] },
    {96,  100, frames[3] },
    {101, 110, frames[2] },
    {111, 115, frames[1] },
    {116, 200, frames[0] },
    {201, 205, frames[7] },
    {206, 210, frames[8] },
    {211, 215, frames[9] },
    {216, 220, frames[10] },
    {221, 225, frames[11] },
    {226, 230, frames[12] },
    {231, 235, frames[13] },
    {236, 240, frames[14] },
    {241, 245, frames[15] },
    {246, 250, frames[16] },
    {251, 255, frames[17] },
    {256, 260, frames[18] }
}
```

If you look at the graphics, you will see there are actually two kinds of animations there. One where the object is mocking us and the other when the object was hit. We added both of them to the MovieClip instance and now we need to separate them. So, at first touch ball will only mock us, and would display the hit animation only after it was hit.

To do that, we can define go to actions. So when the animation reaches the end frame of the last image of the first animation, we need to automatically jump to the first frame of the first image of the same animation. In our case the end frame of the first animation is 200; so from 200 we need to jump to first frame, which can be done using the setGotoAction() method.

Then do the same to the second animation which ends at the 260th frame and starts at the 201st frame.

```
self.bitmap:setGotoAction(200, 1)
self.bitmap:setGotoAction(260, 201)
```

Now we need to create a method for `TouchBall` class to change the animation from first one to the second one. To do this, we will use the `gotoAndPlay` method, which will simply go to the frame number 201 and start to play from it, thus looping in the second animation.

```
function TouchBall:hit()
  self.bitmap:gotoAndPlay(201)
end
```

As the last thing, we need to call the newly created method for `TouchBall` when it is hit. Thus, let's go to `LevelScene.lua` and call `bodyA.object:hit()` inside the `onBeginContact` method, right after we make main ball smile.

Now if you launch the project and try it out, you will see that at first touch ball is mocking us; and after a hit, it gets its eyes spinning.

Tweening elements with GTween

We learned the first type of animation, that is, frame animation; let's now try and tween something. **Tweening** or interpolation is the process of generating animation frames between the two states of the animation. For example, if we want to animate an object moving from one coordinate to other, we could simply set the target coordinate and tween this object using specific tweening library. This would automatically change coordinates step-by-step to provide the animation until it reaches the target coordinate. In Gideros it is possible to tween all sprite inherited object's properties, such as coordinates, scaling, and alpha values among others.

We could also tween objects using `MovieClip` and this is very helpful when you have a framed animation that also needs to be tweened. But if you want to tween one simple `sprite` inherited object, there is no need to use `MovieClip`; you can simply use the `GTween` library for that purpose.

You can get the latest GTween version for Gideros at `https://github.com/gideros/GTween`.

Simply copy `gtween.lua` to your project and add it to the `classes` folder inside Gideros Studio.

Then, to tween any `sprite` inherited object you simply call `GTween.new` and provide the `sprite` object, animation time, and target properties that have to be animated. For example, if a sprite is currently positioned at coordinates (10, 10) and alpha value 0.5, and we want to animate it to the coordinates (100, 100) with alpha value 1 and we want the animation to last 10 seconds, we could call the `GTween` class like this: `GTween.new(sprite, 10, {x=100, y=100, alpha=1})`.

So, we will, emphasize the hit of the touch ball in our game by shaking the screen a little bit using the `GTween` class. For this purpose, let's create a `shakeScreen` method inside the `LevelScene` class, where we first put the scene at coordinate (-10,-10) and then tween it back to coordinate (0,0) in half a second. We will also use `easing.outBounce` as the easing function to add even more bounciness to the shake.

```
function LevelScene:shakeScreen()
  self:setPosition(-10, -10)
  GTween.new(self, 0.5, {x = 0,y = 0}, {delay = 0, ease =
    easing.outBounce })
end
```

Let's call the `shakeScreen` method right after we change animation of hit touch ball inside the `onBeginContact` method.

```
if bodyA.type == "touch" and bodyB.type == "main" then
  --smile
  bodyB.object:smile()
  bodyA.object:hit()
  self:shakeScreen()
end
```

Now, the first time main ball hits each touch ball, it will also give an additional shake effect to the whole screen to emphasize the hit.

 To sum it up, you should use MovieClip if you want to use frame animations. Use GTween if you want to animate some properties of the element. Although MovieClip also provides tweening, GTween provides a much cleaner approach with options to chain tweens, reset and invert values, and others that MovieClip does not offer.

Improving gameplay

There are a lot of ways to improve the player experience, starting from the gameplay of the game logic itself to polishing the interface of the rest of the game scenes. It was difficult to decide what exactly to include showing some cool improvements. So, I decided to make one improvement to the pack selection. This improvement will allow switching between packs using swipe gesture. And there are also other improvements to show you how to implement the key element of Mashballs game, controlling main ball using touch input in a magnet-like style..

Changing level packs by using the swipe gesture

Currently we can only switch the packs by clicking on the corresponding button. But for most of the mobile users, it might seem pretty natural to switch these kinds of screens by swiping their finger to the left or right direction. Let's implement this for user's convenience.

Starting with MouseDown

Let's start with a handle for the MOUSE_DOWN event. Inside it we will set the self.isFocus property so we would know that we are interacting with the scene currently. We will also store the current click's x coordinate inside self.startX, then the current scene's x position inside self.initX, and the previous x coordinate in self.prevX (which in this case will be the same as self.startX). We also call event:stopPropagation() to stop the propagating event.

```
function LevelSelectScene:onMouseDown(event)
    self.isFocus = true
    self.startX = event.x
    self.initX = self:getX()
    self.prevX = event.x
    event:stopPropagation()
end
```

Continue with MouseMove

Now we need to handle the MOUSE_MOVE event where we will move the scene on the x axis. So, at first we check if we are interacting with this scene by checking the self.isFocus flag. Then we calculate the distance we moved the cursor/finger and store it in variable dx. After that we increase the scene's position by dx. Thus, it gets moved with the cursor/finger. Then we set the current event coordinates as self.prevX so that we can use it in the next mouse move iteration, and then we stop the propagation of event.

```
function LevelSelectScene:onMouseMove(event)
  if self.isFocus then
    local dx = event.x - self.prevX
    self:setX(self:getX() + dx)
    self.prevX = event.x
   event:stopPropagation()
  end
end
```

Ending with MouseUp

The most complicated part comes, when we release the scene, inside MOUSE_UP event when we release the scene. In this event we need to determine if we should switch the scene to the next or previous one, or if the change was so small that we need to put the scene back to its place.

```
function LevelSelectScene:onMouseUp(event)
end
```

So again we check the self.isFocus flag first to see if we are interacting with the scene. Then we create a back variable to indicate whether we should put the scene back and set its default value to false.

```
if self.isFocus then
    local back = false
end
```

In the if statement we check if we have moved the scene at least 10 pixels to the left side by checking the start coordinates inside self.startX and the last coordinates in self.prevX and subtracting 10.

```
if self.startX < self.prevX - 10 then
```

If it is `true`, we check if current pack is not the first pack and there is something to show. If there is another pack before, we call `self:prevPack()` (the method we created before). This will switch the scene to previous pack. Else we set variable back to `true` to put the scene back.

```
if self.curPack > 1 then
  self:prevPack()
else
  back = true
end
```

If we did not move the scene to the left side, we need to check if we have moved it to the right-side again by comparing `self.startX` and `self.prevX`, and this time we add 10 pixels.

```
elseif self.startX > self.prevX + 10 then
```

If the scene was moved to the right, we first check if current pack is not the last and call `self:nextPack()` if it's not, else we set `back` variable to `true`.

```
if self.curPack <= #packs then
  self:nextPack()
else
  back = true
end
```

Then we handle the default case. If we have not moved the scene 10 pixels to the right or the left side, we simply set back to `true`.

```
else
  back = true
end
```

In the end we check if `back` is `true`; if yes, we simply tween the scene to its initial position that we stored inside the `self.initX` property. Then we simply set `self.isFocus` flag to false and stop propagation of the event.

```
if back then
  GTween.new(self, 0.1, {x = self.initX})
end
self.isFocus = false
event:stopPropagation()
```

Adding event listeners

As we will be handling input events and dragging the scene, we should wait for the transition between scenes to end so that it won't mess up scene positions. So, at first let's define a new method `LevelSelectScene:onEnterEnd()` inside the `LevelSelectScene.lua` file, which will handle the end of transition event. Inside this method we will add all our mouse event listeners.

```
function LevelSelectScene:onEnterEnd()
  self:addEventListener(Event.MOUSE_DOWN, self.onMouseDown, self)
  self:addEventListener(Event.MOUSE_MOVE, self.onMouseMove, self)
  self:addEventListener(Event.MOUSE_UP, self.onMouseUp, self)
end
```

Then we can add the `onEnterEnd()` method as the event listener to the scene transition inside the `LevelSelectScene:init()` method.

```
self:addEventListener("enterEnd", self.onEnterEnd, self)
```

Modifying code for selecting levels

Currently swiping packs should work on the plain scene without buttons, but as you remember we also have level buttons on this scene. As they are added to the scene, (they are above the scene on z axis) their click events will be called first, which could disrupt our pack switching. So we need to go back to `LevelSelectScene`, the part of the code, where we handle, level's button-click event and modify it. Let's check there if we moved the scene and enter the level only if the scene was not moved.

For a better control of event, we will modify each level button so it won't use our `Button` class but rather the plain `MOUSE_UP` event. Thus, we directly create the `Bitmap` object and add event to it. Additionally we save the reference to the scene for each level image.

```
level = Bitmap.new(Texture.new("images/level_unlocked.png", true))
level.id = i
level.scene = self
```

Then, we check if scene does not have the `startX` property defined inside the click event handler; or if it was moved less than 10 pixels, we can change the scene to the level we clicked.

```
level:addEventListener(Event.MOUSE_UP, function(self, e)
  if self:hitTestPoint(e.x, e.ý) then
    if not self.scene.startX or math.abs(self.scene.startX - e.x) <=
10 then
    sets:set("curLevel", self.id)
```

```
        sceneManager:changeScene("level", conf.transitionTime, conf.
transition, conf.easing)
      end
    end
end, level)
```

Now you can go launch the project and try out switching the packs by a swipe.

Implementing Mashballs magnet

One of the key game elements in Mashballs is the ability to, well not really change, but rather affect the trajectory of the main ball by touching the screen. So, the main ball will get towed to the touch point as affected by some kind of magnetic force.

So let's go to LevelScene.lua and implement it. First we need a method to handle the MOUSE_DOWN events. In this event we will check if MainBall object, which was stored in the self.mainBall property, already has a defined body (which would mean that we already launched the ball). Then, we need to check if the game is not paused; and if it is not paused, we simply set the flag that we start the magnet by setting self.magnetStart flag as true and storing the current magnet's x and y coordinates, whether user touched it.

```
function LevelScene:onMouseDown( event )
  if self.mainBall.body then
    if not self.paused then
      self.magnetStarted = true
      self.magnetX = event.x
      self.magnetY = event.y
    end
  end
end
```

On the MOUSE_MOVE events we check if the magnet is started by checking the self.magnetStarted flag and change the magnet's coordinates to new ones.

```
function LevelScene:onMouseMove( event )
  if self.magnetStarted then
    self.magnetX = event.x
    self.magnetY = event.y
  end
end
```

If the magnet is working in the MOUSE_UP event, we simply take off the flag by setting self.magnetStarted to false.

```
function LevelScene:onMouseUp( event )
  if self.magnetStarted then
    self.magnetStarted = false
  end
end
```

The last thing we need to do here is add these event listeners to the scene inside the LevelScene:init() method.

```
self:addEventListener(Event.MOUSE_DOWN, self.onMouseDown, self)
self:addEventListener(Event.MOUSE_MOVE, self.onMouseMove, self)
self:addEventListener(Event.MOUSE_UP, self.onMouseUp, self)
```

Now we need to affect the main ball when the magnet is enabled. We want to do this by applying a little impulse on each ENTER_FRAME event so that it would give a more natural magnet-like effect. To accomplish that, we will go the MainBall.lua file and add new method there: MainBall:onEnterFrame() method.

Inside it, we will check if the magnet is started by checking the magnetStarted property of the scene reference that was stored inside the self.level property of the MainBall class.

```
function MainBall:onEnterFrame()
  if self.level.magnetStarted then
  end
end
```

Then, we define constant force by which we affect main ball inside the if statement,. On x axis it will simply be 1; but on the y axis, 1 is too big for the force value as it will allow to bring the ball up even if it is sitting still on the floor and is not moving anymore. So, the player could fly the ball in any direction and easily complete the level.

To make the game more interesting, we set a different force to y axis. I found that 0.6 seems to be just the value to allow bringing the ball up using its inertia, but does not allow to move the ball on the y axis if it is sitting still and does not have any additional force to it.

You may experiment more with these values to achieve the exact behavior you wish.

```
local xForce = 1
local yForce = 0.6
```

Then, we need to check the position of the magnet by comparing it to the position of the main ball. If the position of the magnet is lower than the ball's position, it means the magnet is higher than the ball and we need to invert the force to make it bring the ball upwards rather than downwards.

```
if self.level.magnetY < self:getY() then
  yForce = -yForce
end
```

Quite a similar situation also comes up with the x axis. If the magnet's x position is smaller than the ball's position, it means that the magnet is on the the ball's left side and again we need to invert the force that we will apply on the x axis.

```
if self.level.magnetX < self:getX() then
  xForce = -xForce
end
```

Now that we have taken positions into consideration, we can simply apply the force as linear impulse to the current ball's coordinates.

```
self.body:applyLinearImpulse(xForce, yForce, self:getX(),
  self:getY())
```

Last thing to do is to add the onEnterFrame method as event listener to the ENTER_FRAME event inside the MainBall:init() method.

```
self:addEventListener(Event.ENTER_FRAME, self.onEnterFrame, self)
```

Now you can launch the project, open any level, and after launching the ball try to affect its trajectory by using the magnetic force from your own finger tips.

Summary

We have enhanced our game with more stylish controls, such as using swipe gesture on packs and controlling the main game element with a magnetic force created by our own fingers touching the screen. We have also gamified our game with high scores and added tweens and frame animations to juice it up; and let's not forget background music and sounds that we added to complement our game.

Now the game itself is far from finished. But, by now you have learned all the basics that you need to create a game using Gideros. You have also learned about the additions that you can do to improve it visually, acoustically (aurally), and aesthetically.

Index

Symbols

:methodName() method 42
.new() method 42

A

About button
  creating, steps 53
about scene
  creating 55-58
AboutScene:init() method 56
AboutScene class 55
about This Game scene 57
addEventListener method 45, 46, 52
add method 112
Add New File dialog 11
AlertDialog object 104
animated game elements
  creating 118
  elements, tweening with GTween 121, 122
  frame animations, creating with MovieClip 118-121
application:exit() method 54
application:getLogicalScaleX() method 39
application:getLogicalScaleY() method 39
application:getLogicalTranslateX() method 39
application :getLogicalTranslateY() method 39
automatic scaling
  ignoring, for positions 38-41
Autorotation 32

B

b2.DYNAMIC_BODY value 78
b2.setScale(scale) method 79
b2.STATIC_BODY constant 83
b2.STATIC_BODY value 88
Back button 57, 93
background music
  adding 108-111
back variable 124, 125
BEGIN_CONTACT event 117
beginPath() method 73
Bitmap class 42, 44
Bitmap object 44, 72, 88, 96, 126
bodyA.object:hit() method 121
bodyB property 91
bottomLayer variable 20
Box2D 75
Box2D collisions
  handling 88-91
button:setPosition(x,y) method 45
Button class
  about 43-47, 51, 52, 126
  creating 43-47
Button instance 72
Button object 110, 114

C

ChainShape object 83
Change it button 63
changeScene method 48, 49
click event 47, 114

closeMenu() method 75
Code Dependencies 54
coding pane 10
conf.dx offset 74
conf.dy offset 74
config.dx variable 72
config.dy variable 72
Core.class() function 43
Create directory for project option 70
createLevel method 115
curCol counter 96
currentX position 96
currentY position 96

D

dataSaver module 60
DebugDraw layer 76
Deftone Stylus 51
device player installation
  Android player, installing 25
  iOS player, installing 25, 26
  project, running 26, 27
dispatchEvent method 47
Documents directory 60-62, 99

E

e:stopPropagation() method 73
elements
  tweening, GTween used 121, 122
endPath() method 73
ENTER_FRAME event 81, 84, 128, 129
event:stopPropagation() method 47, 123
EventDispatcher class 46, 108
event listeners
  adding 126
Event object 47
Export Project dialog 28
Export Project option 28

F

Filling Ipad zone 39
first project
  creating 10-27

frame animations
  creating, MovieClip used 118-121

G

GameManager:createLevel method 116
GameManager:setScore method 118
GameManager class
  about 99-102, 115, 116
  creating 98-101
GameManager method 115
gameplay
  improving 123
gameplay improvement
  level packs, changing with swipe gesture 123-127
  Mashballs magnet, implementing 127-129
gamification 107
Gideros
  about 6
  Box2D collisions, handling 88-91
  features 6
  installing, on Linux 9
  installing, on Windows 8
  installlling 7
  physical bodies, creating 76-80
  physical bodies, interacting with 83-87
  physics, using in 75, 76
  physics world boundries, setting up 83
  physics world, running 80-82
Gideros API Reference
  URL 5
Gideros class
  creating 43-47
Gideros Community Forum
  URL 5
Gideros desktop player
  using 12, 13
Gideros Developer Guide
  URL 5
Gideros Developer Wiki
  URL 5
Gideros Documentation
  URL 5
Gideros installation
  on Linux 9

on Mac OS X 9
on Windows 8
software packages 7
system requirements 7, 8
Gideros Knowledgebase (FAQ)
URL 5
Gideros Object Oriented Programming. *See*
Gideros OOP
Gideros OOP 31, 42
Gideros Player
graphical objects, displaying in 13, 14
Gideros project
exporting 27, 28
Gideros scene manager
URL 48
using 47-49
Gideros Studio
coding pane 10
panes 10
trying out 10, 11
GiderosTexturePacker 70
global configuration file
creating 49, 50
gotoAndPlay method 121
graphical objects, displaying in Gideros
Player
about 13, 14
images, displaying 15-17
shapes, drawing 18, 19
Sprite class, using 19, 20
text, displaying 14
Graphics tab 24, 32
GTween
URL 121
used, for elements tweening 121, 122
GTween class 122

H

high scores
adding 115
retrieving 116
updating, on screen 117, 118
highScore variable 116
hitTestPoint method 46

I

init method 43, 50, 60, 68, 76, 92, 99, 108
Input tab 24, 32
IntelliJ IDEA 9
iOS tab 32
isDragged flag 86

K

KeyCode.BACK constant 54
KEY_DOWN event 54, 69

L

level definitions
reading 103, 104
levelNumber 96
level packs
changing, swipe gesture used 123
level packs modifications, swipe gesture
used
event listeners, adding 126
MouseDown, starting with 123
MouseMove, continuing with 124
MouseUp, ending with 125
Previous Code, modifying 126, 127
levels
completing 104, 105
definition, reading 103, 104
GameManager class, creating 98-101
grid, generating 95, 96
LevelSelectScene, creating 92-94
managing 92
unlocked levels logic, implementing 101,
102
LevelScene:back() method 68, 69
LevelScene:closeMenu() method 75
LevelScene:completed() method 104, 114
LevelScene:complete() method 118
LevelScene:createMenu() method 73, 75
LevelScene:init() method 69, 74, 81, 89, 103,
116, 128
LevelScene:onBeginContact() method 90
LevelScene:onEnterFrame event 82

LevelScene:onEnterFrame method 81
LevelScene class 68, 122
LevelScene instance 79
LevelScene option 71
levelselect scene 93, 99, 101
LevelSelectScene:onEnterEnd() method 126
LevelSelectScene:init() method 98, 126
LevelSelectScene:nextPack() method 97
LevelSelectScene:prevPack() method 97
LevelSelectScene class
  creating 92-94
levels grid
  generating 95, 96
  screenshot 95
Linux
  Gideros, installing on 9
loadPack() method 99
LuaGlider 9

M

Mac OS X
  Gideros, installing on 9
magnetStarted property 128
MainBall:createBody() method 85, 86
MainBall:init() method 77, 80, 85, 129
MainBall:onEnterFrame() method 128
MainBall:smile() method 90
MainBall class 77, 88, 90, 128
MainBall object 77, 78
main game scene
  implementing 67-69
  texture packs, using 69, 70
  texture packs, using inside project 72-75
  textures, packing 70, 71
MashballsClone project
  about 32
  position automatic scaling, ignoring 38-41
  scaled graphics, handling with AutoScaling
    33, 34
  setting up 32-41
  whitespaces, handling 34-38
Mashballs magnet
  implementing 127-129
MOUSE_DOWN event
  about 45, 85

starting with 123
mouse input events
  Event.MOUSE_DOWN 45
  Event.MOUSE_MOVE 45
  Event.MOUSE_UP 45
MOUSE_MOVE event
  about 86
  continuing with 124
MOUSE_UP event
  about 45, 86
  ending with 124
MovieClip
  used, for frame animations creating 118-121
MovieClip instance 120
MovieClip.new() method 119
MovieClip object 119
Music:off() method 109
Music:on() method 108
Music class 108, 109, 111, 113
musicOff event 109
musicOn event 108, 109

N

new project. See MashballsClone project
New Project dialog 70
nextPack() method 98

O

onBeginContact instant 117
onBeginContact method 114, 117, 121, 122
onEnterEnd() method 126
onEnterFrame event 81
onEnterFrame method 129
onMouseDown method 85
onMouseMove method 86
onMouseUp method 45, 86
onPostSolve event 117
onPostSolve method 118
Options button 52, 53
options scene
  creating 58, 59
OptionsScene class 58
Options screen 108, 111
Output pane 13, 43, 46, 56

P

packed texture 71
packs
  defining 92
  managing 92
  switching between 97, 98
panes 10
physical bodies
  creating 76-80
  interacting with 83-87
physics
  using, in Gideros 75, 76
physics world
  boundries, setting up 83
  running 80-82
physics world boundries
  setting up 83
Player menu 26
POST_SOLVE event 117
Previous Code
  modifying 126, 127
prevPack() method 98
Project pane 11, 32, 42, 48, 71
Project Properties dialog 21
project settings
  automatic image resolution 23
  automatic scaling 21-23
  input settings 24, 25
  iOS-specific settings 25
  managing 21

R

Resource directory 60
Resume button 75
Retina Display 32

S

Save button 64
save method 62
scaled graphics
  handling, AutoScaling used 33, 34
SceneManager constructor 49
sceneManager instance 48, 56, 68
SceneManager.moveFromLeft transition 97

SceneManager.moveFromRight transition 97
scenes
  about scene, creating 55-58
  creating 41, 42
  Gideros class, creating 43-47
  Gideros OOP 42
  Gideros scene manager 47-49
  global configuration file, creating 49, 50
  options scene, creating 58, 59
  Settings class, creating 61-65
  start scene, creating 50-54
scenes directory 68
self:nextPack() method 125
self:prevPack() method 125
self.ballsLeft property 104, 105
self.body:applyLinearImpulse method 87
self.g property 72
self.g variable 72
self.initX property 125
self.isChanged property 62
self.isFocus flag 124
self.isFocus property 123
self.isOn flag 111
self.level instance property 77
self.level property 128
self.magnetStarted flag 127
self.magnetStart property 127
self.mainBall property 127
self.menu property 74
self.packs property 99
self.paused flag 74, 75
self.score property 118
self.scoreText object 117
self.scoreText variable 116
self.score variable 116
self variable 46
self.world:step() method 81
setAlpha() method 44
setPosition() method 44
setText method 64
Settings class
  about 59, 63, 94-97, 104, 113
  creating 60-65
shakeScreen method 122
shape
  physical properties 78

Shape class 44, 83
shape:beginPath() method 18
shape:closePath() method 18
shape:endPath() method 18
Shape instance 73
shape:LineTo method 18
shape object 18, 73
shape:setFillStyle() method 18
shape variable 18
show method 64
smile() method 91
software packages, Gideros installation
    Gideros Font Creator 7
    Gideros License Manager 7
    Gideros Player 7
    Gideros Studio 7
    Gideros Texture Packer 7
sound:play() method 107
sound effects
    adding 111-115
    complete sound effects 113
    hit sound effects 113
Sound object 108, 112
sounds
    adding 107, 108
    background music, adding 108-111
    sound effects, adding 111-115
Sounds:init() method 111
Sounds class 111
Sounds instance 113
soundsOff event 111
soundsOn event 111
sounds option 114
Sprite class 20, 42, 44
sprite instance 42
Sprite object 44, 47, 81, 122
stage:addChildAt method 20
stage class 44
stage variable 19
startButton event 93
Start Game button 51, 53, 68, 79, 93
start scene
    creating 50-54

StartScene init method 48
startX property 126
strength variable 87
Sublime 9
swipe gesture
    used, for level packs changing 123
swipe gesture used
    MouseUp, ending 125

T

Temp directory 60
TextField class 57, 64
TextField object 44, 52, 56, 96, 110, 114
TextInputDialog instance 64
Texture class 42, 69
Texture.new("image.png") parameter 42
TexturePack class 70, 72
Texture Packer window 70
texture packs
    downsides 69
    using 69, 70
    using, inside project 72-75
texturepacks directory 70, 72
textures
    packing 70-72
TextWrap class
    URL 57
    using 58
TextWrap instance
    creating, steps 58
Timer.delayedCall function 90
TouchBall:createBody() method 88
TouchBall class 88-91
TouchBall object 88, 89
touches events
    Event.TOUCHES_BEGIN 45
    Event.TOUCHES_END 45
    Event.TOUCHES_MOVE 45
TrueType Font file 51
TTFont object 51, 52
Turn off text 110
Turn on text 110
tweening 121

U

unlocked flag 100
unlocked levels logic
  implementing 101, 102
unlocked property 100
usernameText field 64

W

whitespaces
  handling 34-38
Windows
  Gideros, installing on 8
world:createBody method 77
world:step() method 81, 84

X

xVect vector 86

Y

yVect vector 86

Z

ZeroBrane 9

About Packt Publishing

Packt, pronounced 'packed', published its first book "*Mastering phpMyAdmin for Effective MySQL Management*" in April 2004 and subsequently continued to specialize in publishing highly focused books on specific technologies and solutions.

Our books and publications share the experiences of your fellow IT professionals in adapting and customizing today's systems, applications, and frameworks. Our solution based books give you the knowledge and power to customize the software and technologies you're using to get the job done. Packt books are more specific and less general than the IT books you have seen in the past. Our unique business model allows us to bring you more focused information, giving you more of what you need to know, and less of what you don't.

Packt is a modern, yet unique publishing company, which focuses on producing quality, cutting-edge books for communities of developers, administrators, and newbies alike. For more information, please visit our website: www.packtpub.com.

Writing for Packt

We welcome all inquiries from people who are interested in authoring. Book proposals should be sent to author@packtpub.com. If your book idea is still at an early stage and you would like to discuss it first before writing a formal book proposal, contact us; one of our commissioning editors will get in touch with you.

We're not just looking for published authors; if you have strong technical skills but no writing experience, our experienced editors can help you develop a writing career, or simply get some additional reward for your expertise.

Corona SDK Mobile Game Development: Beginner's Guide

ISBN: 978-1-84969-188-8   Paperback: 408 pages

Create monetized games for iOS and Android with minimum cost and code

1. Build once and deploy your games to both iOS and Android

2. Create commercially successful games by applying several monetization techniques and tools

3. Create three fun games and integrate them with social networks such as Twitter and Facebook

Developing Mobile Games with Moai SDK

ISBN: 978-1-78216-506-4   Paperback: 136 pages

Learn the basics of Moai SDK through developing games

1. Develop games for multiple platforms with a single code base

2. Understand the basics of Moai SDK

3. Build two prototype games including one with physics

4. Deploy your game to iPhone

Please check **www.PacktPub.com** for information on our titles

www.ingramcontent.com/pod-product-compliance
Lightning Source LLC
LaVergne TN
LVHW062319060326
832902LV00013B/2300